بِسْمِ اللهِ الرَّحْمٰنِ الرَّحِيمِ

Title: Heaven Explored: A Description of Jannah

ISBN: 978-1-952306-22-8

FIRST EDITION | OCTOBER 2023

Author: SAYYID MUHAMMAD IBN ʿALAWI AL-MALIKI
Translator: AHMAD SHAIST KHAN
Typesetting & Distribution: WWW.SATTAURPUBLISHING.COM

www.imamghazali.co

A Translation of What NO Eye Has Seen

Heaven Explored

A Description of Jannah

Sayyid Muḥammad ibn ʿAlawī al-Mālikī al-Ḥasanī ﷺ

CONTENTS

HEAVEN EXPLORED

—

ABOUT THE AUTHOR

SHAYKH MUḤAMMAD IBN ʿALAWĪ IBN ʿABBĀS ibn ʿAbd al-ʿAzīz al-Mālikī al-Ḥasanī al-Makkī, *Shaykh al-Islām fīl-Balad al-Ḥarām*, the educator of Ahl al-Sunnah and light of the House of the Prophet ﷺ in our time, a major contemporary Scholar of ḥadīth, commentary of Qurʾān, Law, doctrine, *taṣawwuf*, and Prophetic biography (*sīrah*), the most highly respected authority of *Ahl al-Sunnah* in the Mother of Cities, passed away in 1425/2004. Both his father (d. 1971CE) and grandfather were the Imāms and head preachers of the Sacred Mosque in Makkah, as was al-Sayyid Muḥammad himself beginning in 1971 and until 1983, at which time he was barred from office after the publication of his book *Mafāhīm Yajib an Tuṣaḥḥaḥ* ("The Necessary Correction of Various Misconceptions").

Sayyid Muḥammad was educated from childhood by his father in the sources of Islām as well as by other noted Makkan scholars such as Sayyid Amīn Kutbī, Ḥassān Mashshāṭ, Muḥammad Nūr Sayf, Saʿīd Yamānī, al-ʿArabī al-Tubbānī al-Mālikī al-Maghribī (Abū Ḥāmid ibn Marzūq), and others. He received his doctorate in Ḥadīth Studies with the highest merits from al-Azhar of Egypt at the age of twenty-five. He then travelled in the pursuit of ḥadīth studies to North Africa, the Middle East, Turkey, Yemen, and the In-do-Pakistani Subcontinent, obtaining teaching certificates (*ijāzāt*) and chains of transmission from Imām al-Ḥabīb Aḥmad Mash-hūr al-Ḥaddād, Shaykh Ḥasanayn Makhlūf, the Ghumārī family of Morocco, Shaykh Ḍyā' al-Dīn al-Qādirī of Madīna, Mawlānā Zakariyyā Kandihlawī, and numerous others.

Shaykh Muḥammad al-Mālikī has authored many books, treatises, and articles on various topics in the Islamic sciences. Among his most famous works:

– *Abwāb al-Faraj* ("The Gates of Deliverance"),[1] a descriptive manual of supplications and devotions for various occasions from the Qur'ān, the Sunnah, and the Imāms of Islām together with a description of the manners of supplicants. It contains a valuable prescription for reciting the *Fātiḥah* frequently.

– *Al-Anwār al-Bahiyyah min Isrā' wa Mi'rāj Khayr al-Bariyyah* ("The Resplendent Lights of the Night Journey and Ascension of the Best of Creation"),[2] a monograph that collates all the sound narrations of the Prophet's ﷺ night journey and ascension into a single narrative.[3]

– *Al-Bayān wal-Ta'rif fī Dhikrā al-Mawlid al-Sharīf* ("The Ex-po-sition and Definition of the Celebration of the Noble Birth-day"),[4] a concise anthology of texts and poems related to the subject.

---

[1]   Cairo: Dār al-Ja'farī, n.d.

[2]   Second ed. Ryad: n. p., 1998.

[3]   A full translation was published in the *Encyclopedia of Islamic Doctrine* and a revised version was published in 1999 together with the original translation of "The Prophets in *Barzakh*" at Al-Sunna Foundation of America publications.

[4]   Published by the author, 1995.

- *Ḥawl al-Iḥtifāl bi Dhikrā al-Mawlid al-Nabawī al-Sharīf* ("Regarding the Celebration of the Prophet's ﷺ Birthday"),[5] a meticulous summation of the proofs adduced by the scholars for the permissibility of celebrating the *mawlid*.

- *Al-Ḥuṣūn al-Manīʿa* ("The Invincible Forts"), a booklet of personal devotions selected from the Sunna and the practice of the *Salaf*.

- *Huwa Allāh* ("{*He is Allāh*}"), a statement of Sunni doctrine in refutation of the aberrations of anthropomorphism.

- *Khulāṣat Shawāriq al-Anwār min Adʿiyat ul-Sūdat al-Akhyār* ("The Epitome of the Rising Lights Taken From the Supplications of the Elect Masters"), a manual of devotions taken from the Sunna and the Imāms of Islām. It contains, among other precious supplications, the devotion (*ḥizb*) of Imām al-Nawawī which begins with the words:

In the name of Allāh, Allāh is greatest! I say upon myself, my Religion, my spouses, my children, my property, my friends, their Religion and their property, a thousandfold "There is no change nor power except with Allāh the Exalted, the Almighty."

- *Al-Madḥ al-Nabawī Bayn al-Ghuluw wal-Inṣāf* ("The Panegyric of the Prophet ﷺ Between Extremism and Fairness"),[6] a study of the genre with examples from the Qur'ān, ḥadīth, com-mentaries, and poetry showing that praising the Prophet ﷺ is part of the perfection of one's Islām and not, as some enviers have claimed, a contravention of the ḥadīth: "Do not

---

[5]   Tenth edition, Cairo: Dār Jawāmiʿ al-Kalim, 1998. Most of its material was incorporated into the section on the *mawlid* in the *Encyclopedia of Islamic Doctrine*.

[6]   Cairo: Dar Wahdan, n.d.

over-extol me (*lā tuṭrūnī*) the way Christians over-extolled ʿĪsā ibn Maryam ☬; [*i.e.* by divinizing him]."[7]

- *Mafāhīm Yajib an Tuṣaḥḥaḥ*, perhaps the most important contemporary statement of *Ahl al-Sunna* on the "Salafī" heresy. In this book Shaykh Muḥammad ibn ʿAlawī establishes the proofs and positions of the Imāms of *Ahl al-Sunna* on the topics of *taṣawwuf, tawassul*, the Prophet's ☬ intercession, the celebration of his birthday (*mawlid*), the Ashʿarī School, etc. with extensive documentation including the sources claimed as authoritative by the "Salafīs" themselves – Ibn Taymiyya, Ibn al-Qayyim, Ibn ʿAbd al-Wahhāb.

- *Mafhūm al-Taṭawwur wal-Tajdīd fīl-Sharīʿa al-Islāmiyya* ("What is Meant by Growth and Renewal in Islamic Law"),[8]

- *Manhaj al-Salaf fī Fahm al-Nuṣūṣ bayn al-Naẓariyya wal-Taṭbīq* ("The Methodology of the Predecessors in Understanding the Texts: Theory and Practice"), his latest work, a continuation and update of the *Mafāhīm* from which we translated the pre-sent book.

- *Muḥammad al-Insān al-Kāmil* ("Muḥammad the Perfect Human Being" ☬),[9] a comprehensive summary of the Prophet's ☬ attributes in the manner of the books of *shamāʾil*.[10] Its chapters are titled as follows:

---

[7]   Narrated from ʿUmar by al-Bukhārī, Mālik, Aḥmad, and al-Dārimī.

[8]   Tenth ed. Madīna, 1999.

[9]   Fourth ed. Madīna: Mat.ābiʿ al-Rashīd, 1990.

[10]   Cf. Al-Tirmidhī, *al-Shamāʾil*; al-Qāḍī ʿIyāḍ, *al-Shifāʾ*; al-Baghawī, al-Qasṭallānī, *al-Mawāhib al-Lāduniyya* and its commentary by al-Zurqānī; al-Suyūṭī, *al-Khaṣāʾiṣ al-Kubrā* and *al-Riyāḍ al-Anīqa*; Shams al-Dīn Muḥammad ibn Yūsuf al-Shāmī al-Ṣāliḥī, *Subul al-Hudā wal-Rashad fī Sira Khayr al-ʿIbad* compiled from over three hundred sources; al-Nabhānī, *Shawāhid al-Ḥaqq*; Shaykh ʿAbd Allāh Sirāj al-Dīn, *Sayyiduna*

- The Perfection of His Lofty Gifts and Pure Attributes.

- The Perfection of His Immunity From Defects and Question-able Aspects, and His Divine Safeguard from Enemies, Devils, and Offences.

- The Perfection of His Magnificent Manners and Noble Qualities.

- The Perfection of His Illustrious Merits and Peerless Traits.

- The Perfection of His Wisdom in Government and Military Leadership.

- The Perfection of His Conduct in the Administration and Education of the Community, and His Heedful Interaction with Them in General and with His Family and Companions in Particular.

- The Perfection of His Law and Its Fulfillment of Human Needs and Keeping Pace with the Spirit of the Times without Incurring Alteration nor Substitution.

– *Al-Mustashriqūn bayn al-Inṣāf wal-ʿAṣabiyya* ("The Orientalists Between Fairness and Prejudice"),[11] a brief survey of the pitfalls of literature on Islām by non-Muslims.[12]

– *Al-Qawāʿid al-Asāsiyya fī ʿUlūm al-Qurʾān* ("Basic Foundations in the Sciences of the Qurʾān"),[13] a useful primer and introduc-

---

Muḥammad ﷺ ; etc. See al-Sakhāwī's *al-Iʿlān* (p. 90-91).

[11] Jeddah: Maṭābiʿ Sahar, 1982.

[12] See Muḥammad ʿAjāj al-Khaṭīb's *al-Sunna Qabl al-Tadwīn* and the works of Dr. Muṣṭafa al-Sibāʿī, Dr. Nūr al-Dīn ʿItr, Dr. Muṣṭafā al-Aʿẓamī, and Muḥibb al-Dīn al-Khaṭīb's epitome of Ibn al-ʿArabī's *al-ʿAwāṣim min al-Qawāṣim*.

[13] Makkah: Published by the author, 1999.

tion to Dr. Nūr al-Dīn ʿItr's *ʿUlūm al-Qurʾān al-Karīm* ("The Sciences of the Noble Qurʾān").[14]

- *Al-Qawāʿid al-Asāsiyya fī Uṣūl al-Fiqh* ("Basic Foundations in the Principles of the Law"),[15] a useful primer and introduction to Dr. Wahba al-Zuhaylī's two-volume *Uṣūl al-Fiqh al-Islāmī*.[16]

- *Al-Qudwat al-Ḥasana fī Manhaj al-Daʿwa ilā Allāh* ("The Excellent Examplar in the Method of Calling Others Unto Allāh").[17]

- *Qul Hādhihi Sabīlī* ("{*Say: This Is My Way*} (12:108)"), a concise manual of Islamic doctrine and morals.

- *Al-Risālat al-Islāmiyya Kamāluhā wa-Khulūduhā wa-ʿĀlamiyyatuhā* ("The Message of Islām: Its Perfection, Immortality, and Universality").[18]

- *Shifāʾ al-Fuʾād bi-Ziyārati Khayr al-ʿIbād* ("The Healing of Hearts Concerning the Visitation of the Best of Human Beings") which establishes the proofs and positions of the Imāms of *Ahl al-Sunnah* on the subject of travelling to visit the Prophet ﷺ in order to obtain blessings (*tabarrukan*) and inter-cession (*tashaffuʿan*).

- *Al-Ṭāliʿ al-Saʿīd al-Muntakhab min al-Musalsalāt wal-Asanīd* ("The New Moon of Happiness: A Selection of Similarly-Narrated Ḥadīths and Chains").[19]

---

14   Sixth ed. Damascus: Maṭbaʿat al-Sabāḥ, 1996.

15   Makkah: Published by the author, 1999.

16   Damascus: Dār al-Fikr, 1986.

17   Tenth ed. Madīnah, 1999.

18   Ed. Najih Maymūn al-Indonisi. Jeddah: ? Maṭābiʿ Sahar, 1990.

19   Second ed. Makkah: Maṭābiʿ al-Ṣafā, 1992.

- *Tārīkh al-Ḥawādith wal-Aḥwal al-Nabawiyyah* ("Historical Events and Markers in the Prophet's 🕌 Life").[20]

- *Al-'Uqūd al-Lu'lu'iyya bil-Asānīd al-'Alawiyya* ("The Pearl Necklaces: 'Alawī's Transmission Chains"),[21] in which the Shaykh lists the transmission chains he received from his father, Sayyid 'Alawī ibn 'Abbās.

- *Wa-Huwa bil-Ufuq al-A'lā* ("{*When He was on the uppermost horizon*} (53:7)"),[22] the most comprehensive commentary to date on the Prophet's 🕌 night journey and ascension, summing up over forty works devoted to the subject. A companion to the Shaykh's al-Anwār al-Bahiyya, the book contains a detailed commentary of the verses that pertain to the vision of Allāh and a full documentation of the authentic relevant narrations.

Sayyid Muḥammad ibn 'Alawī was dearly loved by the people of Makkah, Madinah, and the Ḥijāz. After his forced retirement from public teaching and preaching, he devoted himself to the private education of hundreds of students in Islamic studies, with emphasis on South-East Asian nationals, at his residence and mosque on al-Mālikī street in the Ruṣayfa district of Makkah. Dr. Zuhayr Kutbī of Makkah wrote his biography which was published in Egypt in 1995.[23]

---

20   Twelfth ed. Jeddah: Maṭābi' Sahar, 1996.

21   Second ed.

22   Cairo: Dār Jawami' al-Kalim, 1999.

23   Thanks to Shaykh Fakhroddin Owaisī al-Madanī for some of the above notes.

FOREWORD

Within the domain of Islamic spirituality and eschatology, the concept of Paradise (Jannah) occupies a central place, embodying the ultimate promise and the weightiest ambitions of the faithful. From the works of the late Muḥaddith of Mecca, Sayyid Muhammad ʿAlawī al-Mālikī ﷺ, is a small yet dense work entitled *What No Eye Has Seen*. It is a seminal work that elucidates the celestial abode from an Islamic perspective, and it is our great pleasure and honour to be asked to provide this foreword. With His infinite knowledge, Allah ﷻ is aware that the work you hold in your hand has been translated with meticulous care by Shaykh Ahmad Shaist, our dear and beloved brother and teacher on the Path to Allah. This work of Sayyid Muhammad invites readers to survey their limited understanding of a realm that undeniably transcends human perception and experience.

Allah ﷻ declares in Sūrah al-Tawbah:

وَعَدَ ٱللَّهُ ٱلْمُؤْمِنِينَ وَٱلْمُؤْمِنَٰتِ جَنَّٰتٍ تَجْرِى مِن تَحْتِهَا ٱلْأَنْهَٰرُ خَٰلِدِينَ فِيهَا وَمَسَٰكِنَ طَيِّبَةً فِى جَنَّٰتِ عَدْنٍ وَرِضْوَٰنٌ مِّنَ ٱللَّهِ أَكْبَرُ ذَٰلِكَ هُوَ ٱلْفَوْزُ ٱلْعَظِيمُ ۝

"God has promised the believers, both men and women, Gardens graced with flowing streams where they will remain; good, peaceful homes in Gardens of lasting bliss; and – greatest of all – God's good pleasure. That is the supreme triumph."[1]

The Qur'an expressively describes Paradise as an abode of un-imaginable beauty and eternal bliss, where rivers of milk, honey, and wine flow beneath verdant gardens, whereby all desires are instantaneously fulfilled. It is an eminent plane where the physical and spiritual pleasures are presented in abundance to the righteous, who were able to succeed in the trials of earthly life. These narratives, while offering a glimpse into the Hereafter, serve a greater purpose in the Islamic ethos. They are not mere promises of material reward but also signify a deeper, spiritual fulfilment – the ultimate closeness to Allah, the Exalted.

In this sacred realm, the soul finds its true sanctuary, released from the worldly shackles of pain, sorrow, and despair. The Islamic depiction of Paradise is unique in its emphasis on both spiritual and physical gratification, which in turn reflects the holistic view of human well-being in the religion. In the other-worldly dimension, the dichotomy of body and soul finds a harmonious resolution, and the faithful are rewarded in a manner that befits their earthly endeavours and spiritual purity.

The greatest spiritual pleasure in Paradise will be to see Allah, the Exalted.

لِّلَّذِينَ أَحْسَنُوا۟ الْحُسْنَىٰ وَزِيَادَةٌ وَلَا يَرْهَقُ وُجُوهَهُمْ قَتَرٌ وَلَا ذِلَّةٌ أُو۟لَٰٓئِكَ أَصْحَٰبُ الْجَنَّةِ هُمْ فِيهَا خَٰلِدُونَ ۝

---

1 *al-Tawbah*, 72.

"Those who do good will have the finest reward[2] and more[3]. Neither gloom nor disgrace will cover their faces. It is they who will be the residents of Paradise. They will be there forever."[4]

Sayyid Muhammad ʿAlawī al-Mālikī's work delves into these vivid descriptions, drawing from the rich corpus of the Qur'an and Hadith. It is through the Qur'an that Muslims have come to know of a Paradise where the leaves of the trees are as gentle as the softest silk and where every sense is satisfied with utmost perfection. This work elucidates how these Quranic descriptions are not merely literal but carry deeper allegorical meanings, with each aspect symbolizing a higher spiritual truth or moral virtue.

وَبَشِّرِ ٱلَّذِينَ ءَامَنُوا۟ وَعَمِلُوا۟ ٱلصَّٰلِحَٰتِ أَنَّ لَهُمْ جَنَّٰتٍ تَجْرِى مِن تَحْتِهَا ٱلْأَنْهَٰرُ كُلَّمَا رُزِقُوا۟ مِنْهَا مِن ثَمَرَةٍ رِّزْقًا قَالُوا۟ هَٰذَا ٱلَّذِى رُزِقْنَا مِن قَبْلُ وَأُتُوا۟ بِهِۦ مُتَشَٰبِهًا وَلَهُمْ فِيهَا أَزْوَٰجٌ مُّطَهَّرَةٌ وَهُمْ فِيهَا خَٰلِدُونَ ۞

"Give good news [O Prophet] to those who believe and do good that they will have Gardens under which rivers flow. Whenever provided with fruit, they will say, 'This is what we were given before', for they will be served fruit that looks similar [but tastes different]. They will have pure spouses, and they will be there forever."[5]

---

2 Paradise.

3 Having the honour of glancing at the Countenance of Allah.

4 *Yūnus*, 26.

5 *al-Baqarah*, 25.

Through his profound insights, Sayyid Muhammad ʿAlawī al-Mālikī ﷼, a personal friend of my[6] grandfather Ḥabīb ʿAlī bin ʿĪsā al-Ḥaddād, offers a comprehensive view of these paradisiacal concepts, thereby enriching the reader's understanding of the spheres of theology and spirituality. His work is a beacon for those seeking to comprehend the profound mysteries of the Hereafter. This translation by our dear and beloved brother, Shaykh Ahmad Shaist, constitutes a solemn invitation to the English-speaking Muslim community to reflect on the ephemeral nature of this worldly life and the enduring nature of the life to come.

In a world increasingly driven by materialism and immediate gratification, *What No Eye Has Seen* presents a refreshing viewpoint. In reality, it instils hope and provides solace, offering a glimpse into the divine promise that awaits the faithful.

May Allah bless the invaluable contributions of Sayyid Muhammad ʿAlawī al-Mālikī ﷼ as well as Shaykh Ahmad Shaist for translating this seminal work. His meticulous translation has rendered the profound insights of Sayyid Muhammad ʿAlawī al-Mālikī ﷼ to be accessible to a broader audience, thereby enriching the readership of English-speaking Muslims.

In closing, we offer some advice shared to us by the great caller to Islam in our age, namely Ḥabīb ʿUmar bin Ḥafiḍh, on entering Paradise with the Beloved of Allah ﷺ:

> *People will enter Paradise in groups, one after the other, but there will be a group that enters with him. Most of the people in that group will be from the early generations. Yet, in every cohort, there are people who will be in that group: "In every generation of my Ummah there are those who outstrip others."*

---

6   The grandfather of Zain al-Haddad, co-author of this foreword.

The Prophet ﷺ will enter Paradise and then he will come out again to intercede for various people. He will cause entire groups to enter Paradise.

In the present, people have many conversations and exchanges about the future, but this is the greatest future that is awaiting us. If we were aware of these events, we would not be deceived by anyone.

People compete with each other to have their name written in different places, but it is his name ﷺ that is inscribed upon the Throne. Who inscribed it there? With Whose name is his? Allah placed his name next to His to illustrate his greatness. Whoever lives on the face of the Earth not knowing the greatness of Muhammad ﷺ is at a loss; such a person is undoubtedly distant from his Lord.

If you wish to drink from his Pool in the next life, then drink from the pool of attachment to him in this life, the pool of following him, the pool of his knowledge, the pool of his guidance, and the pool of nurturing your children according to his noble path. If your children taste the sweetness of the connection to him and love for him, they will be safe from all types of tribulation.

May Allah's prayers and peace be upon our Master Muhammad, his Family, and his Companions.

– JOINTLY –
[Shaykh] Musab Penfound
& Sayyid Zain al-Haddad
29 Rabī' al-Ākhir 1445

A Translation of What NO Eye Has Seen

Heaven Explored
A Description of Jannah

Sayyid Muḥammad ibn ʿAlawī al-Mālikī al-Ḥasanī

Introduction

Praise is due to Allah ﷻ, Lord of the Worlds. May blessings and peace be upon the most noble of Messengers, our Master Muhammad ﷺ, and upon his Family ﷺ, and all his noble Companions ﷺ.

To proceed:

This is a short treatise on Paradise and the reports that pertain to it. We have quoted Hadiths without mentioning their chains of transmission or classifying them, relying instead on the sources we have consulted, which include *Ḥādī al-Arwāḥ* by Shaykh Ibn al-Qayyim ﷺ, *Ḥādī al-Anām* by Shaykh al-Mullā ﷺ, *al-Targhīb wa al-Tarhīb* by Imam al-Mundhirī ﷺ, and other books of the Sunnah.

We ask Allah ﷻ that He benefits people through this treatise and that He makes this endeavour purely for His noble Countenance. *Āmīn.*

Written by
Sayyid Muhammad ibn ʿAlawī al-Mālikī al-Ḥasanī ﷺ
The Servant of Sacred Knowledge in the Two Holy Sanctuaries

مقدمة

الحمد لله رب العالمين، والصلاة والسلام على أشرف المرسلين؛ سيدنا محمد وعلى آله وصحبه أجمعين.

أما بعد:

فهذه رسالة مختصرة عن الجنة وما ورد فيها، اعتمدنا فيها على الأحاديث التي أوردناها محذوفة الأسانيد والدرجات؛ اكتفاء بأصولها؛ ككتاب الشيخ ابن القيم «حادي الأرواح»، وكتاب الشيخ الملا «حادي الأنام»، وكتاب المنذري «الترغيب والترهيب»، وغير ذلك من كتب السنة.

نسأل الله تعالى أن ينفع بها، وأن يجعلها خالصة لوجهه الكريم، آمين.

وكتبه
السيّد محمّد بن علوي المالكي الحسني
خادم العِلم الشّريف بالحرمين الشّريفين

The Gates of Paradise

Allah ﷻ states, 'And those who were mindful of their Lord will be led to Paradise in [successive] groups. When they arrive at its [already] open gates, its keepers will say, "Peace be upon you! You have done well, so come in, to stay forever."'[1]

He ﷻ also said, 'the Gardens of Eternity, whose gates will be open for them.'[2]

It has been recorded in authentic Hadiths narrated by the Two Shaykhs[3] ﷺ that there are eight gates to Paradise through which people who [consistently] carried out a particular deed will be summoned to enter, through the gate assigned for that deed.

For example, people who fast consistently will have a specific gate called al-Rayyān that they will enter on the Day of Resurrection. No other people will enter it alongside them. After being summoned and asked, 'Where are the fasting people?' they will enter through this gate. When the last of them has entered, the gate will be closed so that no one else will be able to enter.

There is another gate called al-Ḍuḥā. On the Day of Resurrection, a summoner will proclaim, 'Where are those that consistently prayed the Ḍuḥā prayer? This is your gate, so enter it by the mercy of Allah ﷻ.'

There is another gate specifically for anyone who feeds a hungry believer until they are satiated.

---

1 *al-Zumar*, 73.

2 *Ṣād*, 50.

3 Imam al-Bukhārī and Imam Muslim ﷺ.

أبواب الجنة

قال الله تعالى: ﴿وَسِيقَ ٱلَّذِينَ ٱتَّقَوۡاْ رَبَّهُمۡ إِلَى ٱلۡجَنَّةِ زُمَرًاۖ حَتَّىٰٓ إِذَا جَآءُوهَا وَفُتِحَتۡ أَبۡوَٰبُهَا وَقَالَ لَهُمۡ خَزَنَتُهَا سَلَٰمٌ عَلَيۡكُمۡ طِبۡتُمۡ فَٱدۡخُلُوهَا خَٰلِدِينَ ٧٣﴾.

وقال تعالى: ﴿جَنَّٰتِ عَدۡنٖ مُّفَتَّحَةٗ لَّهُمُ ٱلۡأَبۡوَٰبُ ٥٠﴾.

ثبت في الحديث الصحيح الذي رواه الشيخان: أن أبواب الجنة ثمانية، ولكل أهل عمل باب من أبواب الجنة، يدعون منه بذلك العمل.

فللصائمين باب خاص يسمى (**باب الريان**)، يدخل منه الصائمون يوم القيامة، لا يدخل معهم غيرهم، يقال: أين الصائمون؟ فيدخلون منه، فإذا دخل آخرهم.. أُغلق فلم يدخل منه أحد.

وهناك باب يقال له: (**الضحى**)، فإذا كان يوم القيامة.. نادى مناد: أين الذين كانوا يديمون على صلاة الضحى؟ هذا بابكم، فادخلوا برحمة الله. وهناك **باب خاص** لا يدخل منه إلا من أطعم مؤمنا حتى يشبعه.

There is a gate specifically for *ṣalāh* to which the people who consistently performed it will be summoned. The people of jihad will be summoned from the Gate of Jihad; those who consistently give in charity will be summoned from the Gate of Charity, and whoever spends consistently from his wealth in the path of Allah ﷻ will be summoned from the Gate of Spending.

Allah ﷻ will honour an elect group of His truthful servants who exhausted themselves in the path of righteousness and performed different types of good deeds by summoning them to every single gate. One such person will be Abū Bakr ﷺ. When he asked the Messenger of Allah ﷺ if anyone would be summoned from every single gate, the Prophet ﷺ replied, 'Yes, and it is my hope that you will be one of them.'

Being summoned to every single gate means that a person will be invited to enter through every single gate, which is done to praise and honour that person. However, the gate through which they will actually enter Paradise will be that of the deed they most stringently adhered to.

Every single one of these gates is opened - even while in the temporal world (*dunyā*) - for people who do specific deeds. Whoever performs ablution in the proper manner and then says, 'I testify that there is no god but Allah ﷻ alone without any partners and that Muhammad ﷺ is His servant and Messenger,' will have all eight gates of Paradise open for them, and will enter whichever one they choose to.

In another narration, the invocation reads 'I testify that there is no god but Allah ﷻ alone without any partners; that Muhammad ﷺ is His servant and Messenger; that Jesus ﷺ is the servant of Allah, the son of His bondmaid, His word that He cast upon Maryam ﷺ of His spirit; and that Paradise is real and Hell is real.'

وهناك **باب للصلاة**، فمن كان من أهل الصلاة.. دعي من باب الصلاة، ومن كان من أهل الجهاد.. دعي من باب الجهاد، ومن كان من أهل الصدقة.. دعي من باب الصدقة، ومن أنفق زوجين من ماله في سبيل الله.. دعي من باب النفقة.

وقد يتفضل الله ﷾ على بعض عباده الصادقين الباذلين أنفسهم في سبيل البر وأنواع الخير، فيدعى من جميع الأبواب، وذلك كأبي بكر الذي قال لرسول الله ﷺ: هل يدعى أحد منها كلها؟ قال ﷺ: «نعم؛ وأرجو أن تكون منهم».

ومعنى (**يدعى منها كلها**) أي: ينادى من جميع هذه الأبواب، وهو دعاء تنويه وإكرام، ثم يدخل من الباب الذي غلب عليه العمل به.

وهذه الأبواب تفتح كلها لبعض أرباب الأعمال في الدنيا؛ فمن توضأ وأسبغ الوضوء ثم قال: أشهد أن لا إله إلا الله وحده لا شريك له وأن محمدا عبده ورسوله.. إلا فتحت له أبواب الجنة الثمانية يدخل من أيها شاء.

وفي رواية: «أشهد أن لا إله إلا الله وحده لا شريك، وأن محمدا عبده ورسوله، وأن عيسى عبد الله وابن أمته، وكلمته ألقاها إلى مريم، وروح منه، وأن الجنة حق، والنار حق».

ومن مات له ثلاثة من الولد دون البلوغ.. تتلقاه أولاده من أبواب الجنة الثمانية، يدخل من أيها شاء. والمرأة إذا صلت خمسها، وصامت شهرها، وحفظت فرجها،

Furthermore, whoever suffers the loss of three children before they reach adulthood will be received by their children from the eight gates of Paradise, and will enter whichever one they choose to.

A woman who offers her five daily prayers, fasts during Ramadan, safeguards her private parts, and obeys her husband will be told, 'Enter whichever of the eight gates of Paradise you wish to.'

Whoever takes financial responsibility for his two daughters, or two sisters, or two paternal aunts, or two maternal aunts will have the eight gates of Paradise opened for him.

Imam Muslim ﷺ has narrated that 'Utbah ibn Ghazwān ﷺ said, 'It was mentioned to us that the distance between the two sides of a gate of Paradise is forty years, and yet there will come a day on which it will be brimming due to overcrowding.'

In another narration the Prophet ﷺ swore, 'By the One to Whom the soul of Muhammad belongs, the distance between the two sides of a gate of Paradise is like the distance between Mecca and Hajar, or the distance between Mecca and Basra.'

Qatādah ﷺ commented on this narration, stating that 'the nature of these gates is such that their exterior can be seen from inside and their exterior can be seen from outside. They speak and can be spoken to, and understand when they are told to open and close.'

وأطاعت زوجها.. قيل لها: ادخلي من أي أبواب الجنة شئت.

ومن كان له ابنتان أو أختان أو عمتان أو خالتان، وعالهن.. فتحت له ثمانية أبواب الجنة. وقد أخرج مسلم عن عقبة بن غزوان قال: (ذكر لنا: أن ما بين المصراعين من مصاريع الجنة مسيرة أربعين سنة، وليأتين عليها يوم وهو كظيظ من الزحام).

وفي رواية: يقول ﷺ: «والذي نفس محمد بيده؛ إن ما بين مصراعين من مصاريع الجنة لكما بين مكة وهجر، أو كما بين مكة وبصرى».

يقول الحسن: (هي أبواب يرى ظاهرها من باطنها، وباطنها من ظاهرها، تتكلم وتكلم، وتفهم ما يقال لها: انفتحي، انغلقي).

The Pleasures of Paradise

In many of its verses, the Noble Qur'an gives us a general description of Paradise. It informs us that Paradise is the Garden of Eternal Residence, the Abode of Eternity, and the Abode of Peace – a place of serenity, fragrance and everlasting bliss – and that it is as vast as the Heavens and the Earth, and prepared for the people of *taqwā* (God-consciousness) for whom its gates will be opened.

Similarly, the Prophet ﷺ spoke about Paradise and provided us with a general description in many Prophetic Hadiths, as well as Divine Hadiths which convey the words of Allah ﷻ. He took an oath by the Lord of the Ka'bah that its pleasures include a shining pearl, a fragrant plant that moves with the wind, a well-built palace, a continuously flowing river, ripe fruit, beautiful spouses, numerous garments, eternal residence in a wholesome abode, fruits and greenery, dyed cloths, and blessings in a lofty, splendid place.

What lies therein cannot be compared to anything in the temporal world. The least of things in Paradise is greater than the greatest thing in the temporal world. In fact, a place in Paradise as small as a whip is better than the temporal world and all that it contains. A place as long as a bow given to an inhabitant of Paradise is better than everything the sun rises or sets upon.

If but a single man from the inhabitants of Paradise were to appear in his attire, finery, and bracelets, he would extinguish the light of the Sun just as the light of the Sun extinguishes the light of the stars.

The human mind cannot comprehend the reality of what that abode contains – its numerous blessings, its generous banquets, the

نعيم الجنة

تحدث القرآن الكريم في كثير من آياته عن الجنة وأوصافها العامة؛ فأخبرنا أنها جنة المأوى، ودار الخلد، ودار السلام، وفيها الروح والريحان، والنعيم المقيم، وأن عرضها السموات والأرض، وهي معدة مهيأة للمتقين، مفتحة لهم الأبواب.

وكذلك تحدث ﷺ عن الجنة وأوصافها العامة في كثير من الأحاديث النبوية والقدسية، وأقسم برب الكعبة أنها نور يتلألأ، وريحانة تهتز، وقصر مشيد، ونهر مطرد، وثمرة نضيجة، وزوجة حسناء جميلة، وحلل كثيرة، ومقام في أبد، في دار سليمة، وفاكهة وخضرة، وحبرة ونعمة، في محلة عالية بهية.

لا تقاس بالدنيا بما فيها، فأقل شيء في الجنة هو أعظم من أعظم شيء في الدنيا، بل إن موضع سوط في الجنة خير من الدنيا وما فيها، وإن قاب قوس واحد من أهل الجنة فيها خير مما طلعت عليه الشمس أو غربت.

ولو أن رجلًا من أهل الجنة اطّلع فبدت زينته وحليته وأساوره.. لطمس ذلك ضوء الشمس، كما طمس ضوء الشمس ضوء النجوم.

ولا يستطيع العقل البشري مهما اتسعت مداركه وآفاقه العلمية أن يتصور حقيقة ما في تلك الدار؛ من أنواع النعم، وموائد الكرم، ولذة النعيم، ومتعة النظر إلى

experience of bliss, the pleasure of gazing upon Allah's noble Countenance, the subtleties of the solace found in the sacred domain – no matter how much its intellectual capacities are exhausted. This is because Allah ﷻ has precluded the possibility of anyone acquiring complete knowledge of the reality of what that adobe contains. Allah ﷻ said, 'No soul can imagine what delights are kept in store for them as a reward for what they used to do.'⁴ This is what the Prophet ﷺ referred to when quoting the Lord of Honour ﷻ as saying, 'I have prepared for My righteous servants that which no eye has seen, no ear has heard, and no human heart has imagined.'

This is why when a person sees that bliss, is submerged in the blessings of the position that Allah ﷻ has prepared for them, and becomes touched by the hue of Paradise, their heart and soul will be filled with resplendence, joy, happiness, and glee. They will forget the suffering, adversity, hardship, and misery they experienced in the temporal world. To such an extent that when they are asked, 'O son of Adam. Did you ever suffer? Did you ever experience adversity?' they will reply, 'By Allah, My Lord. I never experienced any suffering, nor did I face any adversity.'

It is a path for which lives should be sacrificed, souls should be sold, and over which men of conscience should compete. It is the truly valuable commodity that believers should hasten to attain, in the knowledge that he who is fearful sets out at nightfall, and he who sets out at nightfall will surely reach his destination, knowing that the destination of this path is the prized commodity of Allah ﷻ, and that the prized commodity of Allah ﷻ is only Paradise.

The only ones who will reach Paradise, however, are those who have been given protection and divine grace; those who are supported and watched over; those who are neither deceived by the desires

---

4 *al-Sajdah*, 17.

الوجه الكريم، ولطائف الأنس في حظيرة القدس؛ لأن الله تعالى نفى وجود العلم الكامل التام بحقيقة ما في ذلك المقام؛ فقال: ﴿فَلَا تَعْلَمُ نَفْسٌ مَّآ أُخْفِيَ لَهُم مِّن قُرَّةِ أَعْيُنٍ﴾، وهذا هو الذي أشار إليه النبي ﷺ فيما يرويه عن رب العزة جل جلاله: «أعددت لعبادي الصالحين ما لا عين رأت، ولا أذن سمعت، ولا خطر على قلب بشرٍ».

ولذلك: فإن الإنسان إذا رأى ذلك النعيم، وانغمس فيما أعده الله له من خير ومقام، وانصبغ في الجنة صبغة.. يمتلئ قلبه ونفسه بالبهجة والحبور، والفرح والسرور، وينسى ما كان فيه في الدنيا من بؤس وشدة وتعب وضنك؛ حتى إنه ليقال له: يا بن آدم؛ هل رأيت بؤسا؟ هل مر بك شدة؟ فيقول: لا والله يا ربي؛ ما مر بي بؤس قطُّ، ولا رأيت شدة قطُّ.

ففي هذا السبيل تبذل المهج، وتباع الأنفس، ويتسابق المجدون، ولأجل هذه السلعة الغالية يسارع المؤمنون، معتقدين أن من خاف.. أدلج، ومن أدلج.. بلغ المنزل، وأن المنزل هو سلعة الله الغالية، وأن سلعة الله هي الجنة.

فلا يصل إلا الموفق المحفوظ، والمؤيد الملحوظ، الذي لا تغره الشهوات المحيطة بالنار، ولا تضره المكاره التي حفت بالجنة؛ لأن الله لما خلق الجنة.. قال لجبريل: «اذهب فانظر إليها، فذهب فنظر إليها، فقال: أي ربِّ؛ وعزتك؛ لا يسمع بها أحد إلا دخلها..

ثم حفها بالمكاره، ثم قال: يا جبريل؛ اذهب فانظر إليها، فذهب فنظر إليها، ثم جاء

that surround the Fire nor fazed by the difficulties that surround Paradise. After creating Paradise Allah ﷻ said to Jibrīl ﷺ, 'Go and see it.' When he saw it, he said, 'My Lord! By Your Majesty, anyone who hears of it will enter it.' He then surrounded it with adversities and said, 'Jibrīl, go and see it.' When he saw it, he came back and said, 'My Lord, I fear that no one will enter it.'

After creating the Fire, Allah ﷻ commanded, 'Jibrīl, go and see it.' After seeing it, he came back and said, 'My Lord! By Your Majesty, no one that hears of it will ever enter it.' He then surrounded it with desires and said, 'Jibrīl, go and see it.' When he saw it again, he said, 'My Lord! By Your Majesty, I fear that there will be no one except that they will enter it.'

When Allah ﷻ created Paradise, hung its fruits up, and made its rivers gush forth, He looked at it and told it to speak. It said, 'Glad tidings to the one with whom You are pleased. The believers are truly prosperous.' He ﷻ then said, 'No miser will reside in you as My neighbour.'

Only the prosperous will arrive in peace and security, and only the believers will be prosperous – those with whom Allah ﷻ is pleased and who are pleased with Him.

فقال: أي رب؛ لقد خشيت ألا يدخلها أحد.

فلما خلق الله النار.. قال: يا جبريل؛ اذهب فانظر إليها، فذهب فنظر إليها، ثم جاء فقال: أي رب؛ وعزتك؛ لا يسمع بها أحد فيدخلها.

فحفها بالشهوات، ثم قال: يا جبريل؛ اذهب فانظر إليها، فذهب فنظر إليها فقال: أي ربِّ؛ وعزتك؛ لقد خشيت ألا يبقى أحد إلا دخلها.

ولما خلق الله الجنة، ودلى فيها ثمارها، وشق فيها أنهارها.. نظر إليها فقال لها: «تكلمي»، فقالت: طوبى لمن رضيت عليه، قَدْ أَفْلَحَ الْمُؤْمِنُونَ، فقال: وعزتي وجلالي؛ لا يجاورني فيك بخيل».

فلا يصل إليها بسلام وأمان إلا المفلحون، ولا يفلح إلا المؤمنون، الذين رضيَ اللهُ عنهُمْ ورضوا عنه.

Degrees and Stations of Paradise

Since the deeds of people are not all the same, the way they will be honoured and given blessings in the Hereafter will likewise vary. Since this is the case, their stations within Paradise will also be of varying degrees. In this way, the virtue, precedence, and endeavours of the people of merit, perfection, and deeds will be recognised.

The Real ﷻ has informed us in His Mighty Book that there are varying degrees to Paradise. He ﷻ stated, 'Far superior ranks, forgiveness, and mercy from Him. And Allah is All-Forgiving, Most Merciful.[5] He ﷻ also said, 'They each have varying degrees in the sight of Allah. And Allah is All-Seeing of what they do.'[6] He ﷻ likewise said, 'It is they who are the true believers. They will have elevated ranks, forgiveness, and an honourable provision from their Lord.'[7]

He ﷻ has informed us that some people will be superior to others in these ranks, as He ﷻ said, 'Those who stay at home – except those with valid excuses – are not equal to those who strive in the cause of Allah with their wealth and their lives. Allah has elevated in rank those who strive with their wealth and their lives above those who stay behind [with valid excuses]. Allah has promised each a fine reward.'[8]

It has been reported that a person in Paradise will look upwards and see a flash of lightning. He will be taken by surprise and alarm

---

5 *al-Nisā'*, 96.

6 *Āl 'Imrān*, 163.

7 *al-Anfāl*, 4.

8 *al-Nisā'*, 95.

درجات ومراتب

ولما كان الإنعام والإكرام الأخروي في الجنة متفاوتًا؛ لاختلاف أعمال الناس.. اقتضى ذلك أن تكون منازلهم في الجنة أيضا على مراتب مختلفة ودرجات متفاوتة، ليظهر فضل الفاضل، وسبق الكامل، وجهد العامل.

وقد أخبر الحق سبحانه وتعالى في كتابه العزيز أن في الجنة درجات؛ فقال: ﴿دَرَجَٰتٍ مِّنْهُ وَمَغْفِرَةً وَرَحْمَةً وَكَانَ ٱللَّهُ غَفُورًا رَّحِيمًا﴾، وقال: ﴿هُمْ دَرَجَٰتٌ عِندَ ٱللَّهِ وَٱللَّهُ بَصِيرٌۢ بِمَا يَعْمَلُونَ﴾، وقال: ﴿أُوْلَٰٓئِكَ هُمُ ٱلْمُؤْمِنُونَ حَقًّا لَّهُمْ دَرَجَٰتٌ عِندَ رَبِّهِمْ وَمَغْفِرَةٌ وَرِزْقٌ كَرِيمٌ﴾

وأخبر سبحانه وتعالى: أن الناس يزيد بعضهم على بعض في تلك الدرجات؛ فقال: ﴿لَّا يَسْتَوِى ٱلْقَٰعِدُونَ مِنَ ٱلْمُؤْمِنِينَ غَيْرُ أُوْلِى ٱلضَّرَرِ وَٱلْمُجَٰهِدُونَ فِى سَبِيلِ ٱللَّهِ بِأَمْوَٰلِهِمْ وَأَنفُسِهِمْ فَضَّلَ ٱللَّهُ ٱلْمُجَٰهِدِينَ بِأَمْوَٰلِهِمْ وَأَنفُسِهِمْ عَلَى ٱلْقَٰعِدِينَ دَرَجَةً وَكُلًّا وَعَدَ ٱللَّهُ ٱلْحُسْنَىٰ﴾.

وأن العبد ليرفع بصره وهو في الجنة فيلمع له برق، فيتعجب الناظر ويأخذه الفزع من ذلك البرق اللامع الذي كاد يخطف بصره، ويقول ما هذا؟ فيقال: «هذا نور أخيك فلان، فيرى نوره أعظم من نوره، ودرجته أعلى من درجته، فيقول: أخي فلان؟! كنا نعمل في الدنيا جميعا، فكيف قد فضل علي هكذا؟! قال: فيقال له:

at this bright flash of lightning that nearly blinded him. He will ask, 'What is this!?' At once, he will be told, 'This is the light of your brother So-and-so.' When he realises that his brother's light is greater than his own and that his brother's station is higher than his own, he will say, 'My brother So-and-so? We did the same things in the temporal world. Why has he been more honoured than me in this way?' He will be told, 'His deeds were better than yours.' His heart will then be given contentment until he is content.

Another man will enter Paradise with his slave, but his slave will be in a higher station than him. He will complain, 'My Lord, this man was my slave in the temporal world!' He will then be told, 'He remembered Allah ﷻ more than you did.'

There are one hundred levels in Paradise. The distance between each level is the same as the distance between the sky and the Earth. The highest and greatest of these levels is al-Firdaws, from whence the four rivers of Paradise gush forth.

For this reason, the Messenger of Allah ﷺ taught us that whenever we ask Allah ﷻ for Paradise, we should ask for al-Firdaws. He also clarified to us the way we can attain this and reach the highest and most noble of all levels of Paradise, and the doors that will lead us to it. They include 'making ablution in the proper manner, even when it is difficult; by taking many steps to the mosque; and by waiting in anticipation of the next prayer immediately after the previous one.'

There is a special level of Paradise that is exclusively reserved for three types of people: 'a just ruler, a person who maintains his bonds of kinship, and someone who is patient in looking after his dependants.' The way to attain the highest and most exclusive heights of Paradise is, therefore, known. The door leading to them is open, and the path to attain them has been made easy for all those who yearn for them.

إنه كان أفضل منك عملا، ثم يجعل في قلبه الرضا حتى يرضى».

وإن الرجل وعبده يدخلان الجنة، فيكون عبده أرفع درجة منه، فيقول: «يا ربِّ؛ هذا كان عبدي في الدنيا؟! فيقال: إنه كان أكثر ذكرا لله منك».

وفي الجنة مائة درجة، بين كل درجتين كما بين السماء والأرض، وأعلى هذه الدرجات وأعظمها هي الفردوس.

فالفردوس أعلاها درجة، وفوقها عرش الرحمن، ومنها تفجر أنهار الجنة الأربعة.

ولذا: فقد أمرنا رسول الله ﷺ إذا سألنا الجنة أن نسأل الله الفردوس، وبين لنا سبيل إدراك أعلى هذه الدرجات، وطريق الوصول إلى أشرفها، وأبواب الارتقاء فيها؛ وهي: «إسباغ الوضوء على المكاره، وكثرة الخطا إلى المساجد، وانتظار الصلاة بعد الصلاة».

وهناك درجة مخصوصة لا ينالها إلا ثلاثة: «إمام عادل، وذو رحم وصول، وذوعيالٍ صبور».

فمن أحب أن ينال أعلى الدرجات، أو يفوز بتلك الدرجات المخصوصة.. فإن طريقها معروف، وبابها مفتوح، وسبيلها ميسر قريب.

The greater the avidity, endeavour, and effort, the higher the degree of Paradise achieved, the more successful the outcome, the more profitable the trade, the greater the victory, and the more abundant the blessings will be. The reality of this affair will only become evident, and its form will only take shape, in the Afterlife – in the arenas of Divine Pleasure and the presence of the Most Merciful ﷻ, on the day in which those degrees will be a light that shines like dazzling lighting.

Since a believer has high and lofty aspirations and desires, only being satisfied with the best of things and the highest of degrees, it is only natural that his soul will yearn for, aspire to, and be devoted to attaining the highest, most noble, most perfect and loftiest of degrees in Paradise. For this reason, expansive gates of good deeds have been opened for him in the temporal world, so that he can enter them and strive for them. Through them, Allah ﷻ will raise his degrees in Paradise. He will continue to ascend the heights of Paradise until he reaches the lofty station that has been destined for him. Contentment will then be placed in his heart, such that he is content with what he has been given.

These gates include those opened for: performing jihad in the path of Allah ﷻ; memorizing the Qur'an while consistently reciting it; making ablution properly even when it is difficult; taking many steps to the mosque; waiting in anticipation for the next prayer immediately after the previous one; remembering Allah ﷻ abundantly; speaking a good word that a person may not pay attention to yet nevertheless pleases Allah ﷻ and His Messenger ﷺ; displaying beautiful patience in the face of a great and difficult calamity, interceding – in a beneficial way – with a person of authority on someone's behalf in order to repel an undesirable outcome or attain a desirable effect; pardoning someone who has wronged you; giving

وكلما كان الحرص والجد والاجتهاد عظيماً.. كانت الدرجة عالية، والنتيجة ناجحة، والتجارة رابحة، والفوز كبيراً، والخير كثيراً، وهذا لا تظهر حقيقته وتبرز صورته إلا هناك في ساحات الرضوان ورحاب الرحمن، يوم يكون لتلك الدرجات نور يلمع كالبرق الخاطف.

ولما كان المؤمن ذا همة عالية، ورغبة رفيعة غالية، لا يقنع إلا بالمعالي، ولا يرضى إلا بالمراتب العوالي.

كان لا بد أن تتشوق نفسه إلى أعلى هذه الدرجات، وتتوق إلى أشرفها، وتتعلق بأكملها وأرفعها، ولذلك فتحت له في الدنيا أبواب واسعة من صالح الأعمال، يدخل منها ويسعى إليها، فيرفعه الله بها في الجنة درجات يرقى فيها ويرقى حتى يصل إلى المنزلة الرفيعة المقدرة له.

ثم يجعل في قلبه الرضا حتى يرضى.

ومن تلك الأبواب: الجهاد في سبيل الله، وحفظ القرآن مع ملازمة تلاوته، وإسباغ الوضوء على المكاره، وكثرة الخطا إلى المساجد، وانتظار الصلاة بعد الصلاة، والإكثار من ذكر الله، وكلمة طيبة ترضى الله ورسوله، يتكلم بها الرجل من رضوان الله لا يلقي لها بالا، وصبر جميل على بلاء مكروه عظيم، وشفاعة حسنة عند ذي سلطان في دفع مكروه أو مبلغ بر، وعفو عمَّن ظلم، وإعطاء لمن حرم، ووصل لمن قطع.

generously to someone who has deprived you; and connecting with a relative who has cut ties with you.

There are certain degrees that Allah ﷻ has reserved for particular people, such that no other people save those who have performed these very deeds can attain these degrees. For example, there is a special degree that is only attained by those who are overcome with worries about earning a lawful livelihood for their dependants.

وقد اختص الله سبحانه وتعالى بعض الناس بدرجات معينة لا ينالها غيرهم، ولا يدركها إلا من عمل بعملهم؛ فهناك درجة مخصوصة لا ينالها إلا أرباب الهموم والتفكير في السعي على العيال بالحلال.

Description of the Gates of Paradise

There is a special gate reserved for this Ummah, such that it is the only Ummah to enter through this gate. The Musnad contains a Hadith narrated by Ibn 'Umar ﷺ, in which the Prophet ﷺ said, 'The width of the gate through which my Ummah will enter Paradise is the same distance a fast rider travels in three periods.[9] However, there will be so much congestion at this gate that their shoulders will almost pop out of their sockets.' In another Hadith narrated by Abū Hurayrah ﷺ, the Prophet ﷺ said, 'Jibrīl came to me, took me by my hand, and showed me the gate of Paradise through which my Ummah will enter.'

Abū Hurayrah ﷺ said,

I placed a pot of *tharīd* and meat in front of the Messenger of Allah ﷺ. He took the shoulder, as it was his favourite part of the goat. After taking a bite, he ﷺ said, 'I will be the master of all people on the Day of Resurrection.' He took another bite and said, 'I will be the master of all people on the Day of Resurrection.' When he saw that his Companions were not questioning him about this, he said, 'Do you not ask how?' So they asked, 'How?' He replied, 'All of humanity will stand in front of the Lord of the Worlds. They will all hear the summoner, and they will all be seen…'

Abū Hurayrah ﷺ continued and narrated the entire Hadith of the Intercession, at the end of which the Prophet ﷺ states:

---

9 Some commentaries of this Hadith say this means three days and nights, while others suggest it means three years.

صفة أبواب الجنة

ولهذه الأمة باب مختص بهم يدخلون منه دون سائر الأمم، كما في «المسند» من حديث ابن عمر عن النبي ﷺ قال: «باب أمتي الذين يدخلون منه الجنة: عرضه مسيرة الراكب المجود ثلاثا، ثم انهم ليضغطون عليه حتى تكاد مناكبهم تزول».

وفيه من حديث أبي هريرة عن النبي ﷺ: «أتاني جبريل، فأخذ بيدي، فأراني باب الجنة الذي تدخل منه أمتي... » الحديث.

وعن أبي هريرة ﵁ قال: وضعت بين يدي رسول الله ﷺ قصعة من ثريد ولحم، فتناول الذراع - وكان أحب الشاة إليه - فنهش نهشة وقال: «أنا سيد الناس يوم القيامة».

ثم نهش أخرىٰ وقال: «أنا سيد الناس يوم القيامة»، فلما رأى أصحابه لا يسألونه.

قال: «ألا تقولون: كيفه؟»

قالوا: كيفه؟ قال: «يَقُومُ النَّاسُ لِرَبِّ الْعَالَمِينَ، فيسمعهم الداعي، وينفذهم البصر... »

I will go forth until I am at the base of the Throne and will fall down in prostration to my Lord. The Lord of the Worlds will then appoint me to a station to which He had never previously appointed anyone else, nor to which He will ever appoint anyone else to thereafter. I will then say, 'My Lord; my Ummah, my Ummah!' He will respond by saying: 'O Muhammad, admit those of your Ummah who have no account to give through the Right Gate (al-Bāb al-Ayman). They will also share access to all the other gates alongside the rest of humanity.'

'Alī ibn Abī Ṭālib ﷺ narrated that the Prophet ﷺ said, 'The gates of Paradise are, in this manner, one on top of another.' He then recited the verse 'when they arrive at its already opened gates'[10] and said:

There they will find two flowing springs at the base of a tree. They will drink from one of these springs, which will expel any trace of impurity or harm from their stomachs. They will bathe in the other spring, which will cause the glow of delight (naḍrah al-naʿīm) to flow through them, causing their heads to never become dishevelled and their skins to never change ever again.

He then recited, 'You have done well, so come in, to stay forever'[11] and said:

A person will then enter Paradise knowing where his house is. His servants will receive him and rejoice at seeing him, just as one's family members rejoice when an intimate relative returns after an absence. The servants will go to inform their spouses that they have seen their master, to which the spouses will exclaim, 'You saw him?' and go to the main door. He will enter his house and recline on his bed. When he looks at the foundations of the house, he will see that they are built on pearls. He will see green, red, and yellow. He will then raise his head to look at the ceiling of his house. Were it not

---

10 *al-Zumar*, 73.

11 *al-Zumar*, 73.

فذكر حديث الشفاعة بطوله، وقال في آخره: «فأنطلق فآتي تحت العرش، فأقع ساجدا لربي، فيقيمني رب العالمين مقاما لم يقمه أحدا قبلي، ولن يقيمه أحدا بعدي، فأقول: يا رب؛ أمتي أمتي، فيقول: يا محمد؛ أدخل من أمتك من لا حساب عليهم من الباب الأيمن، وهم شركاء الناس فيما سوى ذلك من الأبواب».

وعن علي بن أبي طالب رضي الله عنه قال: (إن أبواب الجنة هكذا بعضها فوق بعض).

ثم قرأ: ﴿حَتَّىٰٓ إِذَا جَآءُوهَا وَفُتِحَتْ أَبْوَٰبُهَا﴾.

(إذا هم عندها بشجرة في أصلها عينان تجريان، فيشربون من إحداهما؛ فلا تترك في بطونهم قذىً ولا أذىً إلا رمته، ويغتسلون من الأخرىٰ، فتجرى عليهم نضرة النعيم؛ فلا تشعث رؤوسهم، ولا تتغير أبشارهم بعد هذا أبدا).

ثم قرأ: ﴿طِبْتُمْ فَٱدْخُلُوهَا خَٰلِدِينَ﴾.

(فيدخل الرجل وهو يعرف منزله، وتتلقاهم الولدان فيستبشرون برؤيتهم كما يستبشر الأهل بالحميم يقدم من الغيبة، فينطلقون إلى أزواجهم، فيخبرونهن بمعاينتهم، فتقول: أنت رأيته؟ فتقوم إلى الباب، فيدخل إلى بيته فيتكيء إلى سريره، فينظر إلى أساس بيته؛ فإذا هو قد أسس على اللؤلؤ، ثم ينظر في أخضر وأحمر وأصفر، ثم يرفع رأسه إلى سمك بيته، فلولا أنه خلق له.. لالتمع بصره، فيقول: الحمد لله الذي هدانا لهذا، وما كنا لنهتدي لولا أن هدانا الله).

for the fact that the house had been created for him, it would have blinded him. He will then say, 'Praise be to Allah for guiding us to this. We would have never been guided if Allah had not guided us.'

Allah ﷻ describes 'the Gardens of Eternity, whose gates will be open for them. There they will recline, calling for abundant fruit and drink.'[12] There is a profound symbolism in this verse in that, when they enter Paradise, its gates will not be closed after they enter. Rather, they will remain open as they are.

On the other hand, when the inhabitants of the Fire enter the Blaze, its gates will be closed after them. Allah ﷻ states, 'It will be sealed over them'[13], meaning that its gates will be closed. In the Arabic language, the word 'threshold' (*mu'ṣadah*) is also used to refer to a door. This door is described as 'tightly secured' with long braces.[14] The long braces will hold the doors tightly from behind, just as a huge boulder is used to secure a door shut.

The great exegete Muqātil ﷺ said, 'The doors will be securely shut behind them, not a single door ever being opened again. No sorrow will be able to leave, and no respite will ever be able to enter.'

In addition, the fact that the gates of Paradise will remain open means that people will be able to do as they will, going and coming, and settling wherever they wish to within Paradise. Angels will also be able to come in at any time, bearing gifts and benevolence from their Lord, as well as other things that will bring the inhabitants of Paradise joy.

This is also an indication of the fact that Paradise is a place of security. They will not need to close the gates as they would have been compelled to do in the temporal world. Muqātil ﷺ said, 'Since the

---

12   *al-Zumar*, 50-51.

13   *al-Humazah*, 8.

14   *al-Humazah*, 9.

وفي قوله سبحانه وتعالى: ﴿جَنَّـٰتِ عَدۡنٍ مُّفَتَّحَةً لَّهُمُ ٱلۡأَبۡوَٰبُ ۞ مُتَّكِـِٔينَ فِيهَا يَدۡعُونَ فِيهَا بِفَـٰكِهَةٍ كَثِيرَةٍ وَشَرَابٍ ۞﴾ معنى بديع ورائع؛ وهو أنهم إذا دخلوا الجنة.. لم تغلق أبوابها عليهم، بل تبقى مفتحة كما هي.

وأما النار: فإذا دخلها أهلها.. أغلقت عليهم أبوابها كما قال الله تعالى: ﴿إِنَّهَا عَلَيۡهِم مُّؤۡصَدَةٌ ۞﴾؛ أي: مطبقة مغلقة، ومنه سمي الباب وصيدا، وهي مؤصدة، ﴿فِي عَمَدٍ مُّمَدَّدَةِۭ ۞﴾ قد جعلت العمد ممسكة للأبواب من خلفها؛ كالحجر العظيم الذي يجعل خلف الباب.

قال مقاتل: (يعني أبوابها عليهم مطبقة، فلا يفتح لها باب، ولا يخرج منها غم، ولا يدخل فيها روح آخر الأبد).

وأيضا: فإن في تفتيح الأبواب لهم إشارة إلى تصرفهم وذهابهم وإيابهم، وتبوئهم من الجنة حيث شاؤوا، ودخول الملائكة عليهم في كل وقت بالتحف والألطاف من ربهم، ودخول ما يسرهم عليهم في كل وقت.

وأيضا: إشارة إلى أنها دار أمن لا يحتاجون فيها إلى غلق الأبواب كما كانوا يحتاجون إلى ذلك في الدنيا،

قال فيه: (ولما كانت الجنان درجات بعضها فوق بعض.. كانت أبوابها كذلك، وباب الجنة العالية فوق الجنة التي تحتها، وكلما علت الجنة...

gardens of Paradise are of differing levels, one on top of another, its gates are likewise the same. The gate of the highest level of Paradise is directly above the gate of the level beneath it. The higher the level of Paradise, the wider it is. Every level is more vast than the one below it. The width of the gate of each level depends on the size of the Heaven itself. This is possibly the reason why there is a difference of opinion over the distance between the two sides of the gates of Paradise. Some gates are higher – and therefore wider – than others.'

اتسعت، فعاليها أوسع مما دونه، وسعة الباب بحسب سعة الجنة. ولعل هذا وجه الخلاف الذي جاء في مسافة ما بين مصراعي الباب؛ فإن أبوابها بعضها أعلى من بعض).

The Ground, Soil, and Gravel of Paradise

Abū Hurayrah ﷺ narrated:

We said, 'O Messenger of Allah, tell us about Paradise and its buildings.' He replied, 'They are made of bricks of gold and silver, whose mortar will be a strong-scented musk; its gravel will be made up of pearls and sapphires, while its soil will be saffron. Whoever enters it will live happily and never be sad, living eternally and never dying. His clothes will never wear out, and his youthfulness will never wane.'

Abū Hurayrah ﷺ also narrated that the Prophet ﷺ said:

The ground of Paradise is white, while its open spaces will be composed of boulders of camphor. There will be musk everywhere, billowing like sand dunes, and it will contain never-ending rivers. When the inhabitants of Paradise – the first and the last – convene and get to know one another, Allah ﷻ will send forth a wind of mercy that will awaken and stir up the scent of that musk. When one of them returns home to his spouse, his scent and appearance will be more pleasant than when he had left her. She will say, 'I was already attracted to you when you left, but now I am even more attracted to you.'

Anas ibn Mālik ﷺ narrated that Abū Dharr ﷺ used to say that the Messenger of Allah ﷺ said, 'When I entered Paradise, I saw canopies of pearls, and its ground was of musk.' In another narration, he ﷺ described its soil as being similar to 'fine white powder, pure musk.'

أرض الجنة وترابها وحصباؤها

عن أبي هريرة ﵁ قال: قلنا: يا رسول الله؛ حدثنا عن الجنة ما بناؤها؟ قال: «لبنة من ذهب، ولبنة من فضة، وملاطها المسك الأذفر، وحصباؤها اللؤلؤ والياقوت، وترابها الزعفران.. من يدخلها، من يدخلها.. ينعم لا يبأس، ويخلد لا يموت، لا تبلى ثيابه، ولا يفنى شبابه».

وعن أبي هريرة ﵁، عن النبي ﷺ قال: «أرض الجنة بيضاء، وعرصتها صخور الكافور، وقد أحاط بها المسك مثل كثبان الرمل، فيها أنهار مطردة، فيجتمع فيها أهل الجنة؛ أولهم وآخرهم، فيتعارفون، فيبعث الله تعالى ريح الرحمة، فتهيج عليهم ريح ذلك المسك، فيرجع الرجل إلى زوجته وقد ازداد طيبا وحسنا، فتقول: لقد خرجت من عندي وأنا بك معجبة وأنا بك الآن أشد إعجابا».

وعن أنس بن مالك ﵁ قال: كان أبو ذر يحدث: أن رسول الله ﷺ قال: «أدخلت الجنة؛ فإذا فيها جنابذ اللؤلؤ، وإذا ترابها المسك».

وفي رواية: أنه ﷺ قال عن تربتها: إنها «درمكة بيضاء، مسك خالص».

وقد وردت عن نبينا ﷺ أحاديث كثيرة يفيد مجموعها: أن تربة الجنة متضمنة للنوعين: المسك، والزعفران؛ وهذا يحتمل معنيين:

There are many narrations transmitted from the Prophet ﷺ which, when read in conjunction, impart the impression that the soil of Paradise is composed of both musk and saffron. There are two possible explanations for this apparent contradiction. The first interpretation is that the soil (*turāb*) is actually made from saffron, but when it is mixed with water, it becomes musk. In the Arabic language, clay/mud[15] (*ṭīn*) can also be referred to as *turāb*. This explanation is also supported by another narration telling us that the mortar of Paradise is musk, as mortar is essentially clay. This is further supported by the narration of al-'Alā' ibn Ziyād ﷺ, which reads 'its soil is saffron, while its clay is musk.'

In this way, since its soil and water are both fragrant, when they are combined, they form a perfume akin to musk.

The second potential interpretation is that the soil of Paradise is similar to saffron in colour, but like musk in scent. This would entail that it has the best of both qualities, such that it is bright and delightful by being coloured like saffron while carrying the scent of musk.

This is also supported by the fact that the soil of Paradise has also been likened to *darmak*, which is a type of plain bread that is yellowish in hue while being soft to touch.

This secondary explanation has been encapsulated in the report of Sufyān ibn 'Uyaynah ﷺ who narrated from Ibn Abī Najīḥ ﷺ who narrated from Mujāhid ﷺ that 'the ground of Paradise is silver, and its soil is musk', meaning that its colour will be similar to silver while its scent will be akin to musk.

---

15 Translator's note: clay/mud is a mixture of soil and water.

أحدهما: أن يكون التراب من زعفران، فإذا عجن بالماء.. صار مسكا، والطين يسمى ترابا، ويدل على هذا: قوله في اللفظ الآخر: «ملاطها المسك»، و(الملاط): الطين، ويدل عليه: أن في حديث العلاء ابن زياد: «ترابها الزعفران، وطينها المسك».

فلما كانت طينتها طيبة وماؤها طيبا: فإذا انضم أحدهما إلى الآخر.. حدث لهما طيب آخر فصار مسكا.

والمعنى الثاني: أن يكون زعفرانا باعتبار اللون، ومسكا باعتبار الرائحة، وهذا من أحسن شيء؛ تكون البهجة والإشراق في لون الزعفران، والرائحة في رائحة المسك.

وكذلك تشبيهها بالدرمك؛ وهو الخبز الصافي الذي يضرب لونه إلى صفرة، مع لينها ونعومتها.

وهذا معنى ما ذكره سفيان بن عيينة عن ابن أبي نجيح عن مجاهد: «أرض الجنة من فضة، وترابها مسك»؛ فاللون في البياض لون الفضة، والرائحة رائحة المسك.

The Mansions and Palaces of Paradise

The Qur'an tells us about the mansions of Paradise. The Exalted ﷻ declared, 'But those mindful of their Lord will have elevated mansions, built one above the other, under which rivers flow.'[16] The Exalted ﷻ further informed us that 'they will be secure in elevated mansions.'[17] The Exalted ﷻ also promised believers 'splendid homes in the Gardens of Eternity'[18]

The Prophet ﷺ described these homes for us, saying, 'There are mansions in Paradise: their exterior can be seen from inside, and their interior can be seen from outside.' The Companions ﷢ asked, 'Who do they belong to, O Messenger of Allah?' He replied, 'They belong to those whose speech is pleasant, those who feed others, and those who spend the night standing in prayer while people are sleeping.'

This Hadith indicates that such mansions rightfully belong to anyone who possesses these noble characteristics and venerable attributes, namely good character, generosity, steadfastness, and righteousness. These qualities compose a single unit that should be a part of a Muslim's intrinsic disposition in terms of belief, character, and righteousness.

He ﷺ also said, 'The person with the lowest status in Paradise will have a house made from a single pearl. Its chambers and doors will all be made from it.'

---

16 *al-Zumar*, 20.

17 *Saba'*, 37.

18 *al-Tawbah*, 72.

غرف الجنة وقصورها

قد تحدّث القرآن عن غرف الجنة؛ فقال تعالى: ﴿ لَـٰكِنِ ٱلَّذِينَ ٱتَّقَوۡاْ رَبَّهُمۡ لَهُمۡ غُرَفٞ مِّن فَوۡقِهَا غُرَفٞ مَّبۡنِيَّةٞ تَجۡرِى مِن تَحۡتِهَا ٱلۡأَنۡهَٰرُ ﴾.

وقال تعالى: ﴿ وَهُمۡ فِي ٱلۡغُرُفَٰتِ ءَامِنُونَ ﴾.

وقال تعالى: ﴿ وَمَسَٰكِنَ طَيِّبَةً فِي جَنَّٰتِ عَدۡنٍ ﴾.

وأخبر عنها ﷺ فقال: «إن في الجنة غرفا يرى ظاهرها من باطنها، وباطنها من ظاهرها»، قالوا: لمن يا رسول الله؟ قال: «لمن أطاب الكلام، وأطعم الطعام، وبات قائما والناس نيام».

وهذا الحديث يدل على أن هذه الغرف يستحقها من اتصف بتلك الصفات العالية والمناقب السامية؛ من حسن الخلق، وكرم النفس، والاستقامة والصلاح، فهي وحدة واحدة ينبغي أن تتوفر في شخص المسلم عقيدة وأخلاقا وصلاحا.

وقال أيضا: «إن أدنى أهل الجنة منزلا لرجل له دار من لؤلؤة واحدة، غرفها وأبوابها منها».

He ﷺ further clarified which particular categories of people will deserve these mansions and palaces. They will include those who love one another for the sake of Allah ﷻ, as well as those who visit and help one another for His sake. He ﷺ thus declared, 'The mansions in Paradise of those who love one another for the sake of Allah will appear like a rising easterly or westerly star. People will ask, "Who are they?" They will be told, "They are the ones who love one another for the sake of Allah."'

He ﷺ likewise said, 'There are mansions in Paradise, whose exterior can be seen from inside and whose interior can be seen from outside. Allah has prepared them for those who love one another for His sake, those who visit one another for His sake, and those who expend their wealth and efforts for one another for His sake.'

The inhabitants of these mansions also include those who build a mosque; those who pray the twelve units of the Ḍuḥā prayer or pray twelve supererogatory units of prayer throughout the day and night; those who pray the emphatically recommended four units of prayer before Ẓuhr and two units after it, two units after ʿAṣr, two units after Maghrib, and two units before Fajr; those who pray either twenty or ten units of prayer between Maghrib and ʿIshāʾ; and those who enter the marketplace and say:

Lā ilāha illa ʾllāhu waḥdahū lā sharīka lah lahu ʾl-mulku wa lahu ʾl-ḥamd yuḥyī wa yumīt wa huwa ḥayyun lā yamūt biyadihi ʾl-khayr wa huwa ʿalā kulli shayʾin qadīr.

There is no god except Allah alone without partner, Sovereignty is His, Praise is due to Him, He gives life and He gives death, He is the Living and will never die, all good is in His hand, and He is Powerful over all things.

Likewise, such mansions will be granted to those who regularly perform four units of prayer prior to ʿAṣr; those who start their days

وقد بين ﷺ أيضا من يستحق هذه الغرف وتلك القصور؛ فمنهم المتحابون في الله، والمتزاورون والمتعاونون فيه.

قال ﷺ: «إن المتحابين في الله لترى غرفهم في الجنة كالكوكب الطالع الشرقي أو الغربي، فيقال: من هؤلاء؟ فيقال: هؤلاء المتحابون في الله عَزَّ وَجَلَّ».

وقال: «إن في الجنة غرفا يرى ظاهرها من باطنها، وباطنها من ظاهرها، أعدها الله للمتحابين فيه، والمتزاورين فيه، والمتباذلين فيه».

ومنهم:

- «من بنى لله مسجدا».

- و«من صلى صلاة الضحى ثنتي عشرة ركعة».

- و«من صلى ثنتي عشرة ركعة تطوعًا في يوم وليلة».

- و«من صلى أربع ركعات قبل الظهر، وركعتين بعدها، وركعتين قبل العصر، وركعتين بعد المغرب، وركعتين قبل الصبح».

- و«من صلى بين المغرب والعشاء عشرين ركعة».

fasting, accompany a funeral procession, visit a sick person, and feed a needy person; those who regularly recite Sūrah al-Dukhān during the day or night on Friday; and those who recite Sūrah al-Ikhlāṣ ten-fold, which is established by the following narration in which the Prophet ﷺ said:

> Whoever recites Sūrah al-Ikhlāṣ ten times will have a palace built for them in Paradise. Whoever recites it twenty times will have two palaces built for them in Paradise. And whoever recites it thirty times will have three palaces built for them in Paradise.

This reward is likewise conferred on whoever loses their child, yet praises Allah ﷻ, saying *innā lillāhi wa innā ilayhi rājiʿūn* (certainly to Allah we belong and to Him will we all return), which is evident in the following Prophetic narration:

> When a servant's child dies, Allah asks the Angels, 'Did you take the soul of My servant's child?' They will say, 'Yes.' He will ask, 'Did you take [the soul] of the fruit of his heart?' They will say, 'Yes.' He will ask, 'What did My servant say?' They will reply, 'He praised You and said, "Surely to Allah we belong and to Him we will [all] return."' Then Allah will say, 'Build a house for My servant in Paradise and name it the House of Praise.'

One of the Salaf ﷺ said:

> The floors of a building in Paradise are built using *dhikr*. If a person stops making dhikr, the builders will stop building. They will be asked, 'Why have you stopped?' and will reply, 'We cannot build until we have the materials.'

It is reported from al-Ḥasan ﷺ that the Prophet ﷺ said, 'The Angels work for the children of Adam in Paradise, planting and building. If they stop, they are asked why they have stopped. They reply

- و«من ركع عشر ركعات بين المغرب والعشاء».

- و«من دخل السوق فقال: لا إله إلا الله وحده لا شريك له، له الملك، وله الحمد، يحيي ويميت، وهو حي لا يموت، بيده الخير، وهو على كل شيء قدير».

- و«من حافظ على أربع ركعات قبل العصر».

- و«من أصبح صائماً، فشيّع جنازة، وعاد مريضاً، وأطعم مسكيناً».

- و«من قرأ (حمَ الدخان) في ليلة الجمعة، أو يوم الجمعة».

- و«من قرأ (قل هو الله أحد) عشر مرات؛ جاء في الحديث: أن النبي ﷺ قال: «من قرأ (قل هو الله أحد) عشر مرات.. بني له قصر في الجنة، ومن قرأها عشرين مرة.. بني له قصران في الجنة، ومن قرأها ثلاثين مرة.. بني له ثلاثة قصور في الجنة».

- و«من مات له ولد فحمد واسترجع؛ قال ﷺ: «إذا مات ولد العبد.. قال الله لملائكته: قبضتم ولد عبدي؟ فيقولون: نعم، فيقول: قبضتم ثمرة فؤاده؟ فيقولون: نعم، فيقول: ماذا قال عبدي؟ فيقولون: حمدك واسترجع، فيقول الله: ابنوا لعبدي بيتا في الجنة، وسموه بيت الحمد».

قال بعض السلف: (بلغني أن دور الجنة تبنى بالذكر، فإذا أمسك عن الذكر.. أمسكوا عن البناء، فيقال لهم: قد أمسكتم؟ فيقولون: حتى تأتينا نفقة).

that they can only continue when provided with the materials.' To this, al-Ḥasan ﷺ said, 'Let my father and mother be ransomed for you – send them to work!'

The ground of Paradise is like an empty plain, and good deeds are its raw materials. They are used to build palaces and to plant [greenery in] its land. When the planting and building is complete, its residents can move in.

One of the righteous once saw someone in a dream who said to him, 'We have been ordered to finish building your house. Its name is the House of Joy, so rejoice. We have been commanded to fumigate and decorate it. This will take seven days.' He died seven days later and was seen thereafter in a dream in which he said, 'I was admitted to the House of Joy, and I am in a joyful state. Do not ask what is in it! When an obedient person takes residence therein, they will experience generosity the likes of which they will never have previously witnessed.'

وعن الحسن أنه قال: (الملائكة يعملون لبني آدم في الجنان؛ يغرسون ويبنون، فربما أمسكوا، فيقال لهم: ما لكم قد أمسكتم؟ فيقولون: حتى تأتينا النفقات)، فقال الحسن: (فابعثوهم ـ بأبي أنتم وأمي ـ على العمل).

أرض الجنة اليوم قيعان، والأعمال الصالحة لها بنيان، بها تبنى القصور، وتغرس أرض الجنان، فإذا تكامل الغرس والبنيان.. انتقل إليه السكان.

رأى بعض الصالحين في منامه قائلا يقول له: (قد أمرنا بالفراغ من بناء دارك، واسمها دار السرور، فأبشر، وقد أمرنا بتبخيرها وتزيينها، والفراغ منها إلى سبعة أيام، فلما كان بعد سبعة أيام.. مات، فرُئي في المنام فقال: أُدخلت في دار السرور وأنا في سرور، فلا تسأل عما فيها ! لم ير مثل الكريم إذا حلّ به المطيع).

The Scent of Paradise

It is mentioned in a Hadith that 'The scent of Paradise can be smelt from the distance it takes forty years [to travel].' Another narration states 'five hundred years', while yet another states 'seventy autumns'. The differences in these narrations is probably a result of the varying degrees and levels of Paradise.

There are two types of scents in Paradise. One type can be experienced by the soul in the temporal world from time to time, but this experience cannot be explained in physical terms. The other type can be experienced through the physical sense of smell, just as one experiences the scent of flowers and other things. The inhabitants of Paradise will share in their experience of this type of scent in the Hereafter, whether they are near or far. It can also be experienced in the temporal world – with the permission of Allah ﷻ – by the Prophets and Messengers ﷺ, as well as the elect of His servants. It is reported that Anas ibn al-Naḍr ﷺ had such an experience on the Day of Uḥud when he was witnessed proclaiming this very real experience, exclaiming 'How amazing is the scent of Paradise! I can smell it at the foot of Uḥud!'

Allah ﷻ has allowed His servants in this ephemeral world to experience some of the blessings and wonders of Paradise, which include beautiful scents, desirable pleasures, magnificent sights, pleasant fruits, tranquillity, bliss, and the delights of the eye.

Abū Nuʿaym ﷺ related a report by Aʿmash ﷺ from Abū Sufyān ﷺ, who narrated that Jābir ﷺ said that the Messenger of Allah ﷺ said, 'Every single day Allah says to Paradise, "Be fragrant for your

رائحة الجنة

جاء في الحديث: «أن رائحة الجنة توجد من مسيرة أربعين عاما»، وفي رواية: «من مسيرة خمس مئة عام»، وفي رواية: «من مسيرة سبعين خريفا»، ولعل هذا لاختلاف درجاتها وتنوع مراتبها.

وريح الجنة نوعان:

- ريح يوجد في الدنيا تشمه الأرواح أحيانا لا تدركه العبارة.

- وريح يدرك بحاسة الشم للأبدان كما تشم روائح الأزهار وغيرها، وهذا يشترك أهل الجنة في إدراكه في الآخرة، من قرب وبعد، وأما في الدنيا.. فقد يدركه من شاء الله من أنبيائه ورسله وخاصة خلقه، كما جاء: أن أنس بن النضر أدرك ذلك، ووجده في يوم أحد، وكان ينادي ويقول معبرا عن ذلك الشعور الحقيقي: (واهاً لريح الجنة ! أجده دون أحد). وقد أشهد الله سبحانه عباده في هذه الدار آثارا من آثار الجنة، وأنموذجا منها؛ من الرائحة الطيبة، واللذات المشتهيات، والمناظر البهية، والفاكهة الحسنة، والنعيم والسرور، وقرة العين. وقد روى أبو نعيم من حديث الأعمش، عن أبي سفيان، عن جابر قال: قال رسول الله ﷺ: «يقول الله عَزَّوَجَلَّ للجنة كلَّ يومٍ: طيبي لأهلك، فتزداد طيبا، فذلك البرد الذي يجده الناس بالسحر من ذلك»، كما جعل سبحانه نار الدنيا وآلامها وغمومها وأحزانها مذكرة بنار الآخرة؛ قال تعالى

inhabitants." As a result, it becomes more fragrant. The coolness that people experience at dawn is an effect of that increased fragrance.'

Similarly, the pain, worry, and grief caused by the fire of this world is a reminder from Allah ﷻ of the fire of the Hereafter. Allah ﷻ speaks of the fire of this world, saying 'We have made it as a reminder [of the Hellfire]'[19] The Prophet ﷺ has also informed us that the 'intense heat and cold in this world are from the draughts of Hell.' Since this is the case, He must also show His servants the draughts of Paradise and that which reminds them of it.

The Prophet ﷺ taught us that some types of sinners will be prevented from experiencing and enjoying this scent. This group includes those who slay a non-Muslim living under a covenant (*mu'āhad*) unjustly; those who fail to uphold their responsibilities given by Allah ﷻ; those who seek sacred knowledge for worldly benefits; men who falsely ascribe a lineage to themselves; stingy misers; alcoholics; and those who disobey their parents or sever their ties of kinship. Likewise, elderly adulterers; those who haughtily drag their lower garments upon the floor; and women who ask their husbands for a divorce without a sound reason belong in this group.

---

19 *al-Wāqi'ah*, 73.

في نار هذه الدار: ﴿نَحۡنُ جَعَلۡنَٰهَا تَذۡكِرَةٗ﴾، وأخبر النبي ﷺ: «أن شدة الحر والبرد من أنفاس جهنم»، فلابد أن يشهد عباده أنفاس جنته وما يذكرهم بها.

وقد أخبر ﷺ أنه يحرم من هذه الرائحة بعض أرباب المعاصي، فلا يجدونها ولا يتمتعون بها؛ فمنهم:

- «من قتل نفسا معاهدة بغير حقها».
- و«عبد استرعاه الله رعية فلم يحفظها».
- و«رجل تعلم علما ليصيب به عرضا من الدنيا».
- و«رجل ادعى إلى غير أبيه».
- و«المنان، والعاق لوالديه، ومدمن الخمر».
- و«قاطع الرحم».
- و«الشيخ الزاني».
- و«من جر إزاره خيلاء».
- و«امرأة سألت زوجها الطلاق من غير بأس».

The Trees and Shades of Paradise

Allah ﷻ said, 'And the people of the right – how blessed will they be! They will be amid thornless lote trees, clusters of bananas, extended shade, flowing water, abundant fruit – never out of season nor forbidden – and elevated furnishings.'[20]

The Exalted ﷻ also said: 'Both will be with lush branches.'[21] The word used in the verse (*afnān*) is the plural of *fanan,* which means branch. In the same *sūrah,* the Exalted ﷻ also said, 'In both will be fruit, palm trees, and pomegranates.'[22]

The Prophet ﷺ said, 'There is a tree in Paradise so vast that a rider will remain in its shadow for a hundred years without crossing its span. Read the verse "extended shade" if you please.'[23]

He ﷺ also said, 'There is not a single tree in Paradise whose trunk is not made of gold.'

A Bedouin once queried, 'O Messenger of Allah, Allah has mentioned a harmful tree in the Qur'an, while I was of the belief that there would not be any harmful trees in Paradise.' The Messenger of Allah ﷺ replied, 'Allah says, "amid thornless lote trees"[24] – Allah will remove its thorns and replace each thorn with a fruit. It will grow and sprout fruits of seventy-two different colours, with no two colours resembling one another.'

---

20 *al-Wāqiʿah,* 27-34.

21 *al-Raḥmān,* 48.

22 *al-Raḥmān,* 68.

23 *al-Wāqiʿah,* 56.

24 *al-Wāqiʿah,* 28.

أشجار الجنة وظلالها

قال الله تعالى: ﴿وَأَصْحَٰبُ ٱلْيَمِينِ مَآ أَصْحَٰبُ ٱلْيَمِينِ ۝ فِى سِدْرٍ مَّخْضُودٍ ۝ وَطَلْحٍ مَّنضُودٍ ۝ وَظِلٍّ مَّمْدُودٍ ۝ وَمَآءٍ مَّسْكُوبٍ ۝ وَفَٰكِهَةٍ كَثِيرَةٍ ۝ لَّا مَقْطُوعَةٍ وَلَا مَمْنُوعَةٍ ۝ وَفُرُشٍ مَّرْفُوعَةٍ ۝﴾.

وقال تعالى: ﴿ذَوَاتَآ أَفْنَانٍ﴾، وهي جمع فنن؛ وهو: الغصن.

وقال تعالى: ﴿فِيهِمَا فَٰكِهَةٌ وَنَخْلٌ وَرُمَّانٌ﴾.

وقال ﷺ: «إن في الجنة لشجرة، يسير الراكب في ظلها مئة عام ما يقطعها؛ اقرؤوا إن شئتم: ﴿وَظِلٍّ مَّمْدُودٍ﴾.

وقال: «ما في الجنة شجرة إلا وساقها من ذهب».

وقال أعرابي: يا رسول الله؛ لقد ذكر الله في القرآن شجرة مؤذية، وماكنت أرى أن في الجنة شجرة تؤذي صاحبها.

فقال رسول الله ﷺ: «يقول الله: ﴿فِى سِدْرٍ مَّخْضُودٍ﴾: يخضد الله شوكه، فيجعل مكان كل شوكة ثمرة، إنها تنبت، ثم يتفتق الثمر منها عن اثنين وسبعين لونا من

Abū Hurayrah ﷺ stated:

There is a tree in Paradise called Ṭūbā. Allah will say to it, 'Sprout for my servant whatever he wants.' It will then sprout a horse with the precise bridle, saddle, and specifications that he wished for. It will also sprout a riding camel together with the precise saddle, bridle, and specifications that he wished for, as well as clothes.

Ibn ʿAbbās ﷺ stated:

Extended shade refers to a tree in Paradise with a trunk so vast that a good rider would take a hundred years to ride through its shade in each direction. The inhabitants of Paradise will come to it – the dwellers of mansions as well as others – and begin talking in its shade. Some of them will desire something, remembering the pleasure of the temporal world, upon which point Allah will send a wind from Paradise causing the tree to move and produce all the pleasures of the temporal world.

There is a tree in Paradise whose roots are golden and whose canopies are bejewelled. It is crowned with pearls and sapphires. Its fruits are like the breasts of virgins, softer than butter, and sweeter than honey. Every time a fruit is picked off it, it is replaced with another one. This is the meaning of the Exalted's description 'never out of season nor forbidden.'[25] It belongs to anyone that glorifies Allah ﷻ, praises Allah ﷻ, or exalts Allah ﷻ.[26]

There is a tree in Paradise whose fruit is smaller than a pomegranate but bigger than an apple. Its sweetness is like honeycomb and honey. The fasting person will eat from it on the Day of Resurrection.

---

25   *al-Wāqiʿah*, 33.

26   By saying *subḥān Allāh*, *al-ḥamd li Allāh*, and *Allāhu Akbar*.

الطعام، ما منها لون يشبه الآخر».

يقول أبو هريرة ﵁: (إن في الجنة شجرة يقال لها: طوبى، يقول الله لها: تفتقي لعبدي عما شاء، فتتفتق له عن فرس بلجامه وسرجه وهيئته كما شاء، وتتفتق له عن الراحلة برحلها وزمامها وهيئتها كما شاء، وعن الثياب).

ويقول ابن عباس ﵂: (الظل الممدود: شجرة في الجنة على ساق، قدر ما يسير الراكب المجد في ظلها مئة عام في كل نواحيها، فيخرج إليها أهل الجنة؛ أهل الغرف وغيرهم، فيتحدثون في ظلها، قال: فيشتهي بعضهم، ويذكر لهو الدنيا، فيرسل الله ريحا من الجنة، فتتحرك تلك الشجرة بكل لهو في الدنيا).

وفي الجنة شجرة أصلها من ذهب، وأعلاها من جوهر، مكللة بالدر والياقوت، ثمرها كثدي الأبكار، ألين من الزبد، وأحلى من العسل، كلما جُز منها شيء.. عاد مكانه، هذا معنى قوله تعالى: ﴿لَّا مَقْطُوعَةٍ وَلَا مَمْنُوعَةٍ﴾، وهي لمن يسبح الله تسبيحة أو يحمده تحميدة أو يكبره تكبيرة.

وفي الجنة شجرة ثمرها أصغر من الرمان، وأضخم من التفاح، وعذوبته كعذوبة الشهد، وحلاوته كحلاوة العسل، يطعم الله منه الصائم يوم القيامة.

وقد أخبرنا صلوات الله وسلامه عليه: أن كثيرا من أهل الطاعات والأعمال الصالحات ينالون ببركة أعمالهم تلك من الثواب والأجر ما يغرس لهم في الجنة من الأشجار والنخل بلا عد ولا حصر.

The Prophet ﷺ informed us that many of those who were obedient and did good deeds will attain, by the blessings of those deeds, such rewards that will plant for them an immeasurable number of trees including palm trees.

Whoever says, '*Subḥān Allāh al-'aẓīm wa bi ḥamdih* (Glory and Praise be to Allah ﷻ, the Great) will have a palm tree planted for them in Paradise.'

Whoever says, '*Subḥān Allāh wa al-ḥamd li Allāh wa lā ilāha il Allāh wa Allāhu Akbar* (Glory be to Allah ﷻ, Praise is due to Allah ﷻ, there is no god but Allah ﷻ, and Allah ﷻ is the Greatest) will have a tree planted for them in Paradise for every single one of these invocations.'

When a person completes the Qur'an, they are granted an answered prayer, as well as a tree in Paradise. Furthermore, it has been narrated that:

'Whoever fasts an optional day of fasting will have a tree planted for them in Paradise.'

'Whoever walks to his debtor to repay what he owes him, the beasts on the earth and the fish in the sea will pray for him. For every step he takes, a tree will sprout for him in Paradise and his sins will be forgiven.'

فمن قال: «سبحان الله العظيم وبحمده.. غُرس له نخل في الجنة».

ومن قال: «سبحان الله، والحمد لله، ولا إله إلا الله، والله أكبر.. يغرس له بكل واحدة شجرة في الجنة».

- و«عند ختم القرآن دعوة مستجابة وشجرة في الجنة».

- و«من صام يوما تطوعا.. غرست له شجرة في الجنة».

- و«من مشى إلى غريمه بحقه.. صلت عليه دواب الأرض، ونون الماء، ونبتت له بكل خطوة شجرة في الجنة، وذنبه يغفر».

A Description of the Fruits of Paradise
and the Food of its Inhabitants

Allah ﷻ declares, 'There they will have all kinds of fruit.'[27] He ﷻ also states, 'They will have a known provision: fruits of every type. And they will be honoured.'[28]

He ﷻ also promised, 'And We will continually provide them with whatever fruit or meat they desire.'[29] He ﷻ also states, 'And there they will have their provisions morning and evening.'[30]

The Prophet ﷺ informed us that 'no single person in Paradise will pick a fruit except that it will be replaced with the same fruit.' He ﷺ also said that 'a single bunch of grapes in Paradise is as big as the distance between Mecca and Sanaa.' He ﷺ also said that 'a single pomegranate in Paradise is like a hunchbacked camel.'

A man from the People of the Book came to the Messenger of Allah ﷺ and asked, 'O Abū al-Qāsim! You claim that the inhabitants of Paradise will eat and drink?' He ﷺ replied, 'By the One Who possesses my soul, a single man amongst them will be given the strength of a hundred men in food, drink, sexual intercourse, and desire.' The man then asked, 'Will those who eat and drink excrete?' The Prophet ﷺ responded, 'Their excrement will be in the form of sweat that will secrete through their skins like the scent of musk. When he is done, his stomach will shrink back.'

27　*Muḥammad*, 15.

28　*al-Ṣāffāt*, 41-42.

29　*al-Ṭūr*, 22.

30　*Maryam*, 62.

صفة ثمار الجنة وأكل أهلها

قال الله تعالى: ﴿وَلَهُمْ فِيهَا مِن كُلِّ ٱلثَّمَرَٰتِ﴾.

وقال تعالى: ﴿أُوْلَـٰئِكَ لَهُمْ رِزْقٌ مَّعْلُومٌ ۝ فَوَٰكِهُ وَهُم مُّكْرَمُونَ﴾.

وقال عَزَّ وَجَلَّ: ﴿وَأَمْدَدْنَٰهُم بِفَٰكِهَةٍ وَلَحْمٍ مِّمَّا يَشْتَهُونَ ۝﴾.

وقال جل ذكره: ﴿وَلَهُمْ رِزْقُهُمْ فِيهَا بُكْرَةً وَعَشِيًّا﴾.

وأخبرنا ﷺ: «أنه لا ينزع رجل من أهل الجنة من ثمرها.. إلا أعيد في مكانها مثلاها».

- و «أن العنقود من عناقيدها من مكة إلى صنعاء».

- و «أن الرمانة من رمانها مثل البعير المقتب».

وقد جاء رجل من أهل الكتاب إلى رسول الله ﷺ فقال: يا أبا القاسم؛ تزعم أن أهل الجنة يأكلون ويشربون؟ فقال: «والذي نفسي بيده؛ إن الرجل منهم ليؤتى قوة مئة رجل في الأكل، والشرب، والجماع، والشهوة».

The Prophet ﷺ also said, 'The inhabitants of Paradise will eat and drink therein. They will not spit, urinate, defecate, or emit mucus. Their food will be digested into a belch, as well as a secretion like that of musk.' He ﷺ also said:

> The people in the lowest level of Paradise will have ten thousand servants. Every single one of these servants will carry two platters, one of gold and one of silver. Each platter will contain colours that the other one does not. The inhabitant of Paradise will continue eating from the second platter as much as they did from the first, and will experience the same delight from the second platter as they did from the first. It will all then transform into a strong musk. They will not urinate, defecate, or emit mucus. They will be brothers on couches facing each other.

If you see a bird in Paradise that you desire to eat, it will drop in front of you, already grilled, yet no smoke or fire will have touched it. You will eat your fill of it and then it will fly away.

قال: فإن الذي يأكل ويشرب تكون له الحاجة؟ قال: «حاجتهم عرق يفيض من جلودهم مثل ريح المسك، فإذا كان ذلك.. ضمر له بطنه».

وقال ﷺ: «إنَّ أهل الجنة يأكلون فيها ويشربون، ولا يتفلون ولا يبولون ولا يتغوطون ولا يمتخطون، طعامهم جشاء، ورشح كرشح المسك».

وقال: «إن أسفل أهل الجنة أجمعين درجة لمن يقوم على رأسه عشرة آلاف خادم، بيد كل واحد منهم صحفتان، واحدة من ذهب والأخرى من فضة، في كل واحدة لون ليس في الأخرى مثله، يأكل من آخرها مثل ما يأكل من أولها، يجد لآخرها من الطيب واللذة مثل الذي يجده لأولها، ثم يكون ذلك ريح المسك الأذفر، لا يبولون ولا يتغوطون ولا يمتخطون، إخوانا على سرر متقابلين.

وإنك لتنظر إلى الطير في الجنة تشتهيه، فيخر بين يديك مشويا لم يصبه دخان ولم تمسه نار، فتأكل منه حتى تشبع، ثم يطير.

The Rivers of Paradise

Allah ﷻ said, 'Gardens under which rivers flow'.[31]

He ﷻ also stated, 'The description of the Paradise promised to the righteous is that in it are rivers of fresh water, rivers of milk that never changes in taste, rivers of wine delicious to drink, and rivers of pure honey'.[32]

Allah ﷻ mentioned these four types of rivers while negating the possibility of any defect that might spoil any of them in the temporal world. The worldly defect of water is that its odour and taste can change for the worse from stagnation. The defect of milk is that it turns sour and its taste becomes acidic. The defect of wine is that it has an unpalatable taste that reduces the pleasant experience of its consumer. The defect of honey is that it is not purified.

These are some of signs of the Lord ﷻ: He will cause rivers to flow the likes of which do not exist in the temporal world. He will make them flow without any ridges, removing any defects that may prevent one from experiencing full pleasure from them. In addition, He will remove from the wine of Paradise all the defects associated with the wine of the temporal world, such as headaches, nonsensical speech, its finite nature, and unpalatable taste.

These are but a few of the many problems associated with the consumption of wine in the temporal world: it renders the intellect obsolete, increasing nonsensical speech – in fact, those who drink it only find pleasure when this occurs. It decreases with consump-

---

31 *al-Baqarah*, 25.
32 *Muḥammad*, 15.

أنهار الجنة

قال الله تعالى: ﴿جَنَّٰتٍ تَجْرِى مِن تَحْتِهَا ٱلْأَنْهَٰرُ﴾.

وقال تعالى: ﴿مَّثَلُ ٱلْجَنَّةِ ٱلَّتِى وُعِدَ ٱلْمُتَّقُونَ فِيهَآ أَنْهَٰرٌ مِّن مَّآءٍ غَيْرِ ءَاسِنٍ وَأَنْهَٰرٌ مِّن لَّبَنٍ لَّمْ يَتَغَيَّرْ طَعْمُهُ وَأَنْهَٰرٌ مِّنْ خَمْرٍ لَّذَّةٍ لِّلشَّٰرِبِينَ وَأَنْهَٰرٌ مِّنْ عَسَلٍ مُّصَفًّى﴾.

فذكر سبحانه هذه الأجناس الأربعة، ونفى عن كل واحد منها الآفة التي تعرض له في الدنيا، **فآفة الماء:** أن يأسن ويأجن من طول مكثه، **وآفة اللبن:** أن يتغير طعمه إلى الحموضة ويصير قارصا، **وآفة الخمر:** كراهة مذاقها المنافية للذة شربها، **وآفة العسل:** عدم تصفيته.

وهذا من آيات الرب تعالى؛ أن يجري أنهارا من أجناس لم تجر العادة في الدنيا بإجرائها، ويجريها في غير أخدود، وينفي عنها الآفات التي تمنع كمال اللذة بها، كما نفى عن خمر الجنة آفات خمر الدنيا من الصداع والغول، واللغو، والإنزاف، وعدم اللذة. فهذه خمس آفات من آفات خمر الدنيا: تغتال العقل، ويكثر اللغو على شربها، بل لا يطيب لشرابها ذلك إلا باللغو، وتنزف في نفسها، وتنزف المال،

tion, and likewise decreases one's wealth. It causes headaches, and is unpalatable. It is described as 'filth from the work of the Devil' and creates enmity and rancour between people. It prevents one from remembering Allah and prayer. It incites to adultery – in fact, it may even incite one to commit incest with their daughter, sister, and un-marriageable relatives (*maḥrams*) in general! It removes one's protective jealousy (*ghayrah*), and results in humiliation, regret and disgrace. It causes a person to behave like the most helpless of human beings, namely the insane. It strips a person of their best qualities and attributes and gives them the worst of qualities and attributes. It makes it easier to take someone's life, and likewise makes it easier for one to reveal their own secrets, which may lead to their own harm and downfall. It causes one to fraternise with devils and squander the wealth that Allah ﷻ has given them for their maintenance, as well as the maintenance of their dependants. It removes one's inhibitions, exposes their secrets, and points out their weaknesses. It makes it easier for one to commit indecencies and sins and removes the veneration of the sacred from the heart. Its addict is like an idol worshipper.

How many wars has it started! How many wealthy people has it impoverished! How many honourable people has it humiliated, and how many noble people has it debased! How many blessings has it robbed people of, how many misfortunes brought about, how many relationships destroyed, and how many enmities sown!

How many a man has it taken from his beloved, breaking their heart and making them lose their mind! How many a regret has it caused, and how many tears has it caused to flow! How many doors of good has it closed to its consumer and how many doors of evil has it opened!

How often has it caused misfortune and resulted in a premature death! How many a humiliation has it caused, bringing about tribu-

وتصدع الرأس، وهي كريهة المذاق، وهي رجس من عمل الشيطان، توقع العداوة والبغضاء بين الناس، وتصدّ عن ذكر الله وعن الصلاة، وتدعو إلى الزنا، وربما دعت إلى الوقوع على البنت والأخت وذوات المحارم، وتذهب الغيرة، وتورث الخزي والندامة والفضيحة، وتلحق شاربها بأنقص نوع الإنسان؛ وهم المجانين، وتسلب منه أحسن الأسماء والسمات، وتكسوه أقبح الأسماء والصفات، وتسهل قتل النفس، وإفشاء السر الذي في إفشائه مضرته وإهلاكه، ومؤاخاة الشياطين في تبذير المال الذي جعله الله قياما له ولمن يلزمه مؤنته، وتهتك الأستار، وتظهر الأسرار، وتدل على العورات، وتهون ارتكاب القبائح والمآثم، وتخرج من القلب تعظيم المحارم، ومدمنها كعابد وثن.

وكم أهاجت من حرب، وأفقرت من غني، وأذلت من عزيز، ووضعت من شريف، وسلبت من نعمة، وجلبت من نقمة، وفسخت مودة، ونسجت عداوة!

وكم فرقت بين رجل وحبّه، فذهبت بقلبه وراحت بلبه!

وكم أورثت من حسرة، وأجرت من عبرة!

وكم أغلقت في وجه شاربها بابا من الخير، وفتحت له بابا من الشر!

وكم أوقعت في بلية، وعجّلت في منيّة!

وكم أورثت من خزية، وجرت على شاربها من محنة، وجرّأت عليه من سفلة!

lation for its consumer and encouraging him to engage in despicable actions.

It is the accumulator of sin, the key to evil, the plunderer of blessings, and the dealer of misfortunes.

It would be bad enough if its only vice was that it cannot enter the stomach of a person who will consume the wine of Paradise. The Prophet ﷺ declared, 'Whoever drinks wine in the temporal world will not drink it in the Hereafter.'

The problems with wine are many times more than we have mentioned, yet they are all non-existent in the wine of Paradise.

Someone may ask that Allah ﷻ has described the rivers of Paradise as being flowing, and since the odour and taste of flowing water does not change, what is the point of Him describing them as 'fresh'? Even though flowing water does remain fresh, if one was to take some of it out of the river, it would go stale if left to stand for long enough. However, the water in Paradise will not go stale no matter how long it remains still.

Reflect upon the fact that the inhabitants of Paradise will enjoy all four of these rivers, which happen to be the best liquids that people can consume – one for their hydration and purification, one for their strength and nourishment, one for their pleasure and merriment, and one for their healing and benefit.

The Prophet ﷺ has informed us that there are four springs in Paradise. Two of them flow from under the Throne: one of which is described by Allah ﷻ as 'flowing at their will'[33], the other being Zanjabīl.[34]

---

33 *al-Insān*, 6.
34 *al-Insān*, 17.

فهي جماع الإثم، ومفتاح الشر، وسلّابة النعم، وجلابة النقم.

ولو لم يكن من رذائلها إلا أنها لا تجتمع هي وخمر الجنة في جوف عبد.. لكفى، كما ثبت عنه ﷺ أنه قال: «من شرب الخمر في الدنيا.. لم يشربها في الآخرة».

وآفات الخمر أضعاف أضعاف ما ذكرنا، وكلها منتفية عن خمر الجنة.

فإن قيل: فقد وصف الله سبحانه الأنهار بأنهار جارية، ومعلوم أن الماء الجاري لا يأسن، فما فائدة قوله: ﴿غَيۡرِ ءَاسِنٍ﴾.. قيل: الماء الجاري وإن كان لا يأسن؛ فإنه إذا أخذ منه شيء وطال مكثه.. أسن، وماء الجنة لا يعرض له ذلك، ولو طال مكثه ما طال.

وتأمل إجتماع هذه الأنهار الأربعة التي هي أفضل أشربة الناس، فهذا لريهم وطهورهم، وهذا لقوتهم وغذائهم، وهذا للذتهم وسرورهم، وهذا لشفائهم ومنفعتهم.

وقد أخبرنا ﷺ: أن في الجنة أربع عيون:

-عينان تجريان من تحت العرش، إحداهما التي ذكر الله: ﴿يُفَجِّرُونَهَا تَفۡجِيرًا﴾، والأخرى: الزنجبيل.

The other two are gushing springs flowing from above the Throne, one of which is referred to by Allah ﷻ as 'Salsabīl'[35] while the other is named Tasnīm.[36]

He ﷺ also informed us that the rivers of Paradise spurt forth from mountains of musk, and that they flow on the land without any ridges. He ﷺ told us that when a man from the inhabitants of Paradise desires one of the drinks of Paradise, a jug will come to him and fall into his hand. He will drink from it and, when he is done, it will return to its place.

Abū al-Dardā' ﷺ narrated in his exegesis of the verse 'whose last sip will smell like musk'[37] that the Prophet ﷺ said, 'It is a drink that is white like silver. They seal their most treasured drinks with it. If a person from the temporal world were to dip his hand in it and then take it out, there is not a single soul except that it will be able to smell its scent.'

---

35 *al-Insān*, 18.
36 *al-Muṭaffifīn*, 27.
37 *al-Muṭaffifīn*, 26.

- وعينان نضاختان من فوق العرش، إحداهما التي ذكر الله: ﴿سَلْسَبِيلًا﴾، والأخرى: التسنيم.

وأخبرنا: أن أنهار الجنة تتفجر من جبال المسك، وأنها تجري في غير أخدود؛ أي: على وجه الأرض.

وأن الرجل من أهل الجنة ليشتهي الشراب من شراب الجنة، فيجيء الإبريق، فيقع في يده، فيشرب، ثم يعود إلى مكانه.

وعن أبي الدرداء في قوله تعالى: ﴿خِتَامُهُ مِسْكٌ﴾، قال: (هو شراب أبيض مثل الفضة، يختمون به أعز شرابهم، ولو أن رجلا من أهل الدنيا أدخل يده فيه ثم أخرجها.. لم يبق ذو روح إلا وجد ريح طيبها).

The Garments, Jewellery, Furnishings, Couches, and Beds of the Inhabitants of Paradise

The Exalted ﷻ has informed us that the garments of the inhabitants of Paradise are made of fine green silk and rich brocade, as He said, 'And their clothing will be silk.'[38]

He ﷻ further declared, 'There they will be adorned with bracelets of gold, and wear green garments of fine silk and rich brocade, reclining therein on canopied couches.'[39]

He ﷻ also stated, 'The virtuous will be clothed in outer garments of fine green silk and rich brocade, and adorned with bracelets of silver.'[40]

He ﷻ said, 'And elevated furnishings.'[41]

He ﷻ declared, 'Those [believers] will recline on furnishings lined with rich brocades.'[42]

He ﷻ also said, 'They will be maidens with gorgeous eyes, reserved in pavilions.'[43]

Sundus is a type of fine brocade, whereas *istabraq* is a thick type. They are both a type of silk, and the colour green is the best of colours. In this way, the garments of Paradise will be both pleasing to the eye as well as soft to touch.

---

38 *al-Ḥajj*, 23.

39 *al-Kahf*, 31.

40 *al-Insān*, 21.

41 *al-Wāqiʿah*, 34.

42 *al-Raḥmān*, 54.

43 *al-Raḥmān*, 72.

لباس أهل الجنة وحليتهم، وفرشهم، وأرائكهم، وسررهم

أخبرنا ﷾ عن لباس أهل الجنة؛ وأنه من الحرير والسندس الأخضر والإستبرق

فقال: ﴿وَلِبَاسُهُمْ فِيهَا حَرِيرٌ﴾.

وقال: ﴿يُحَلَّوْنَ فِيهَا مِنْ أَسَاوِرَ مِن ذَهَبٍ وَيَلْبَسُونَ ثِيَابًا خُضْرًا مِّن سُندُسٍ وَإِسْتَبْرَقٍ مُّتَّكِئِينَ فِيهَا عَلَى ٱلْأَرَآئِكِ﴾.

وقال: ﴿عَٰلِيَهُمْ ثِيَابُ سُندُسٍ خُضْرٌ وَإِسْتَبْرَقٌ وَحُلُّوٓاْ أَسَاوِرَ مِن فِضَّةٍ﴾.

وقال: ﴿وَفُرُشٍ مَّرْفُوعَةٍ﴾.

وقال: ﴿مُتَّكِئِينَ عَلَىٰ فُرُشٍ بَطَآئِنُهَا مِنْ إِسْتَبْرَقٍ﴾.

وقال: ﴿حُورٌ مَّقْصُورَٰتٌ فِي ٱلْخِيَامِ﴾.

فأما السندس.. فهو ما رق من الديباج، والإستبرق: ما غلظ منه، وهما نوعان من الحرير، واللون الأخضر هو أحسن الألوان، فجمع لهم بين حسن منظر اللباس، والتذاذ العين به، وبين نعومته والتذاذ الجسم به.

Reflect on the fact that they have been described as 'outer' garments. This indicates that these materials will be apparent, beautifying the outer appearance of those who wear them. They will not be akin to a mere lining, but will rather serve as the garments that are worn externally to display one's adornment and beauty.

The context of the verse quoted from Sūrah al-Insān can be interpreted to mean that these garments are actually worn by the youthful servants that will wait on them. However, it can also be interpreted as meaning that these are the garments of the masters whom the youthful servants will wait upon.

Consider also the fact that He ﷻ will adorn them with two types of outer adornments – their garments and jewellery – as well as adorning them both outwardly and inwardly. He will adorn them inwardly by gifting them a Purifying Drink – 'and their Lord will give them a Purifying Drink'[44] – and outwardly by adorning their arms with bracelets – 'and adorned with bracelets of silver'[45] – and their bodies with garments of silk – 'and their clothing will be silk'.[46]

'Abdullāh ibn 'Amr ﷺ narrated that a man asked, 'O Messenger of Allah, tell us about the clothing of the inhabitants of Paradise. Will they be one-piece garments or made from woven fabrics?' Some of those present laughed, at which point the Messenger of Allah ﷺ said, 'What are you laughing at? At someone asking a person of knowledge something he doesn't know?' He then said, 'They will sprout forth from the fruits of Paradise,' twice.

Abū al-Khayr Marthad ibn 'Abdullāh ﷺ narrated that the Prophet ﷺ said, '*Sundus* grows on a tree in Paradise. The garments of the inhabitants of Paradise will be made from it.'

---

44 *al-Insān*, 21.

45 *al-Insān*, 21.

46 *al-Ḥajj*, 23.

وتأمل ما دلت عليه لفظة: ﴿عَلَيْهِمْ﴾ من كون ذلك اللباس ظاهرا، بارزا، يجمل ظواهرهم، ليس بمنزلة الشعار الباطن، بل الذي يلبس فوق الثياب للزينة والجمال.

وقد يكون للولدان الذين يطوفون عليهم، فيطوفون وعليهم ثياب السندس والإستبرق، أو للسادات الذين يطوف عليهم الولدان، فيطوفون على ساداتهم وعلى السادات هذه الثياب.

وتأمل كيف جمع لهم بين نوعي الزينة الظاهرة من اللباس والحلي، كما جمع بين الظاهرة والباطنة، فجمل البواطن بالشراب الطهور فقال: ﴿وَسَقَىٰهُمْ رَبُّهُمْ شَرَابًا طَهُورًا﴾، والسواعد بالأساور فقال: ﴿وَحُلُّوٓا۟ أَسَاوِرَ مِن فِضَّةٍ﴾، والأبدان بثياب الحرير فقال: ﴿وَلِبَاسُهُمْ فِيهَا حَرِيرٌ﴾.

وعن عبد الله بن عمرو قال: قال رجل: يا رسول الله؛ أخبرنا عن ثياب أهل الجنة، أخلق يخلق، أم نسيج ينسج؟ فضحك بعض القوم، فقال رسول الله ﷺ: «مم تضحكون؟ من جاهل سأل عالما؟» ثم قال: «بل تشقق عنها ثمر الجنة مرتين».

وعن أبي الخير مرثد بن عبد الله قال: (في الجنة شجرة نبت السندس، منه يكون ثياب أهل الجنة).

Abū Hurayrah ﷠ narrated that the Prophet ﷺ said, 'The house of a believer will be like a hollowed-out pearl that will comprise of forty apartments. There will be a tree in the middle of it upon which suits of clothing will grow. He will pick, with two fingers, seventy suits decked with pearls, large and small, and chrysolite.'

Abū Saʿīd al-Khudrī narrated that the Prophet ﷺ recited the verse 'They will enter the Gardens of Eternity, where they will be adorned with bracelets of gold and pearls'[47] and then said, 'They will wear crowns, the lowest of whose pearls can illuminate everything between the East and the West.'

The Messenger of Allah ﷺ also said, 'The jewellery with which Allah will adorn the lowest person of the inhabitants of Paradise is better than the jewellery of all the people of the temporal world.'

---

47 *Fāṭir*, 33.

وعن أبي هريرة قال: (إن دار المؤمن درة مجوفة، فيها أربعون بيتا، في وسطها شجرة تنبت الحلل، فيأخذ بأصبعيه سبعين حلة منظمة باللؤلؤ والزبرجد والمرجان).

وعن أبي سعيد الخدري: أن النبي ﷺ تلا قوله تعالى: ﴿جَنَّتُ عَدْنٍ يَدْخُلُونَهَا يُحَلَّوْنَ فِيهَا مِنْ أَسَاوِرَ مِن ذَهَبٍ وَلُؤْلُؤًا﴾، فقال: «إن عليهم التيجان، إن أدنى لؤلؤة منها لتضيء ما بين المشرق والمغرب».

وقال رسول الله ﷺ: «لو أن أدنى أهل الجنة حلية حلية عدلت حليته بحلية أهل الدنيا جميعا.. لكان ما يحليه الله به في الآخرة أفضل من حلية أهل الدنيا جميعا».

Description of the Spouses of Paradise

Regarding spouses of the inhabitants of Paradise, Allah ﷻ says, 'They will have pure spouses.'[48] The word 'pure' here means pure from menstruation, excrement, phlegm, and saliva.

He ﷻ also declared, 'And they will have maidens with gorgeous eyes, like pristine pearls.'[49, 50]

Ḥūr (maidens) is the plural of *ḥawrā'*: a young, beautiful, fair-skinned woman with intensely deep-black eyes. Zayd ibn Aslam ﷺ said, 'A *ḥawrā'* is someone by whom others are mesmerized. *'Īn* refers to women with beautiful eyes.'

Mujāhid ﷺ said, 'A *ḥawrā'* is someone by whom others are mesmerised due to her soft skin and pure complexion.'

Al-Ḥasan ﷺ said, 'A *ḥawrā'* is someone who has eyes, the white parts of which are intensely white and the black parts of which are intensely black.' A woman is only referred to as a *ḥawrā'* if in addition to this attribute regarding her eyes, she is also fair-skinned.

'Īn is the plural of *'aynā'*, which is a word used to describe a woman with large eyes. The preponderant meaning of the word *'īn* is that it refers to women whose eyes contain attributes of beauty and elegance.

Muqātil ﷺ contended that the word *'īn* refers to women with beautiful eyes.

---

48 *al-Baqarah*, 25.

49 *al-Wāqi'ah*, 22-23.

50 Translator's note. The section after this verse is a linguistic explanation of the term of *al-ḥūr al-'īn*, which has been translated in the verse as 'maidens with gorgeous eyes'.

صفة أزواج الجنة

قال الله تعالى في أزواج أهل الجنة: ﴿وَلَهُمْ فِيهَآ أَزْوَٰجٌ مُّطَهَّرَةٌ﴾؛ أي: من الحيض والغائط والنخامة والبصاق.

وقال: ﴿وَحُورٌ عِينٌ ٢٢ كَأَمْثَٰلِ ٱللُّؤْلُؤِ ٱلْمَكْنُونِ ٢٣﴾.

و(الحور): جمع حوراء؛ وهي: المرأة الشابة الحسناء الجميلة البيضاء، شديدة سواد العين.

وقال زيد بن أسلم: (الحوراء: التي يحار فيها الطرف، وعِين: حسان الأعين).

وقال مجاهد: (الحوراء: التي يحار فيها الطرف؛ من رقة الجلد، وصفاء اللون).

وقال الحسن: (الحوراء: شديدة بياض العين، شديدة سواد العين)، ولا تسمى المرأة حوراء حتى تكون مع حور عينها بيضاء لون الجسد.

و(العين): جمع عيناء؛ وهي: العظيمة العين من النساء، والصحيح: أن (العين): اللاتي جمعت أعينهن صفات الحسن والملاحة.

Ibn Mas'ūd ﷺ said, 'The marrow beyond the flesh and bone of the calves of the large-eyed maidens can be seen from under seventy garments just as clearly as one can see a red drink in a clear glass.'

The Exalted ﷻ said, 'In all Gardens will be noble, pleasant mates.'[51]

Khayrāt is the plural of *khayrah,* which is an abbreviated form of *khayyirah,* in the same way that the words *sayyidah* and *layyinah* are also abbreviated. *Ḥisān* is the plural of *ḥasanah* (beautiful). *Khayrāt ḥisān*[52] means that these women have pleasant attributes, amiable characters and dispositions, as well as beautiful faces.

The Exalted ﷻ said, 'They will be maidens with gorgeous eyes, reserved in pavilions'[53] They will be confined to their pavilions, never leaving them. These pavilions will be constructed from pearls and silver.

He ﷻ also said, 'Those maidens will be as elegant as rubies and coral.'[54] The Prophet ﷺ explained the meaning of this verse in his statement:

> When one looks upon her face, he will see that her cheeks are clearer than a mirror. The lowest of the pearls that adorn her will be enough to light up everything between the East and the West. Though she will be adorned with seventy garments, his sight will penetrate these garments so that he will be able to see the core of her calves.

The Exalted ﷻ said, 'In both [gardens] will be maidens of modest gaze,'[55] meaning that their gaze will be limited to their spouses, as

---

51   *al-Raḥmān,* 70. The Arabic phrase here is *'khayrāt ḥisān.'*

52   Referred to the in the translation of the verse 55:70 as 'pleasant mates'.

53   *al-Raḥmān,* 72.

54   *al-Raḥmān,* 58.

55   *al-Raḥmān,* 56.

قال مقاتل: (العين: حسان الأعين).

قال ابن مسعود: (إن المرأة من الحور العين ليرى مخ ساقها من وراء اللحم والعظم ومن تحت سبعين حلة؛ كما يرى الشراب الأحمر في الزجاجة البيضاء).

وقال تعالى: ﴿فِيهِنَّ خَيْرَٰتٌ حِسَانٌ﴾.

و (الخيرات): جمع خيرة؛ وهي مخففة من خيرة؛ كسيدة ولينة، و (الحسان): جمع حسنة، فهي خيرات الصفات والأخلاق والشيم، حسان الوجوه.

وقال تعالى: ﴿حُورٌ مَّقْصُورَٰتٌ فِي ٱلْخِيَامِ﴾؛ أي: محبوسات في الخيام لا يبرحن، والخيمة لؤلؤة وفضة.

وقال: ﴿كَأَنَّهُنَّ ٱلْيَاقُوتُ وَٱلْمَرْجَانُ﴾.

وقد فسّر ذلك صلوات الله وسلامه عليه فقال: «ينظر إلى وجهه في خدها أصفى من المرآة، وإن أدنى لؤلؤة عليها لتضيء ما بين المشرق والمغرب، وإنه يكون عليها سبعون ثوبا ينفذها بصره حتى يرى مخ ساقها من وراء ذلك».

وقال تعالى: ﴿فِيهِنَّ قَاصِرَٰتُ ٱلطَّرْفِ﴾؛ أي: على أ زواجهن، فلا يبغين غير أزواجهنّ.

they will not desire anyone besides them. In the same verse, He ﷻ said 'who no human or jinn has ever touched before.'[56]

The Prophet ﷺ said, 'If a woman of Paradise were to gaze upon the earth, everything in between [her and it] would become illuminated and filled with a breeze. Likewise, the veil on her head is better than the temporal world and all it contains.'

The Prophet ﷺ has also informed us that the inhabitants of Paradise will have multiple spouses. He said, 'There is not a single person in Paradise except that he will have two or more spouses.'

He conveyed to us that these heavenly spouses will convene together every seven days and speak in melodious voices that no creature has ever heard the likes of before:

> We are the eternal ones that will never perish; we are the felicitous ones that will never be miserable; we are the content ones that will never be angered; we are the permanent ones that will never leave. Glad tidings to those who belong to us, and whom we belong to!'

The Messenger of Allah ﷺ said, 'Jibrīl narrated to me and said, "When a man meets his *ḥawrā'*, she will greet him with an embrace and a handshake."'

He ﷺ told us that the inhabitants of Paradise will enjoy sexual relations just as they did in the temporal world, and that a believer will be given the sexual power of a hundred men. He also said that after the inhabitants of Paradise have intercourse with their women, they will become virgins once again, and that, should a man from among the inhabitants of Paradise wish for a child, the entire pregnancy, nursing period, weaning, and youth will take place in a single moment.

---

56 *al-Raḥmān*, 56.

وقال: ﴿لَمْ يَطْمِثْهُنَّ إِنسٌ قَبْلَهُمْ وَلَا جَانٌّ﴾.

قال ﷺ: «ولو أن امرأة من نساء أهل الجنّة اطلعت إلى الأرض.. لأضاءت ما بينهما، ولملأت ما بينهما ريحا، ولنصيفها على رأسها - يعني الخمار - خير من الدنيا وما فيها».

وقد أخبرنا ﷺ عن كثرة أزواج أهل الجنة وقال: «ما في الجنة أحد إلا له زوجتان وأكثر».

وأخبر أنهن يجتمعن في كل سبعة أيام، فيقلن بأصوات حزينة لم يسمع الخلائق بمثلهن: «نحن الخالدات فلا نبيد، ونحن الناعمات فلا نبأس، ونحن الراضيات فلا نسخط، ونحن المقيمات فلا نظعن، طوبى لمن كان لنا وكنا له».

وقال رسول الله ﷺ: «حدثني جبريل قال: يدخل الرجل على الحوراء، فتستقبله بالمعانقة والمصافحة».

وقد أخبرنا ﷺ: أن أهل الجنة يتمتعون بالنكاح كما كانوا يتمتعون به في الدنيا، وأن المؤمن يعطى في الجنة قوة مئة في الجماع، وأن أهل الجنة إذا جامعوا نساءهم، عادوا أبكارا، وأن الرجل من أهل الجنة يتمنى الولد، فيكون حمله ورضاعه وفطامه وشبابه في ساعة واحدة.

It has also been mentioned in a tradition that the inhabitants of Paradise will not experience ritual impurity (*janābah*), weakness, or a refractory period after intimate relations. The intercourse they will enjoy will consist of pure pleasure and comfort without being accompanied or followed by any discomfort.

Those who will experience this in the most complete manner are those who most completely safeguard themselves from the unlawful in this abode. Similarly, anyone who drinks wine in the temporal world will not drink it in the Hereafter; anyone who wears silk in the temporal world will not wear it in the Hereafter; and anyone who eats from dishes of gold and silver will not eat from them in the Hereafter. The Prophet ﷺ said, 'It is for them in the temporal world, but for you in the Hereafter.'

وقد جاء في الآثار: أن أهل الجنة لا تلحقهم الجنابة ولا ضعف ولا إنحلال قوة، بل وطؤهم وطء التذاذ ونعيم، لا آفة فيه بوجه من الوجوه.

وأكمل الناس فيه: أصونهم لنفسه في هذه الدار عن الحرام، كما أن من شرب الخمر في الدنيا.. لم يشربها في الآخرة، ومن لبس الحرير في الدنيا.. لم يلبسه في الآخرة، ومن أكل في صحاف الذهب والفضة.. لم يأكل فيهما في الآخرة، كما قال النبي ﷺ: «إنها لهم في الدنيا ولكم في الآخرة».

The Music of the Inhabitants of Paradise & The Singing of the Large-eyed Maidens

Allah ﷻ said, 'And on the Day the Hour will arrive, the people will then be split into two groups. As for those who believed and did good, they will be rejoicing in a Garden.'[57]

Commentating on the statement of the Exalted ﷻ 'rejoicing in a Garden,' al-Awzāʿī ﷺ said:

> This refers to music. When the inhabitants of Paradise wish to enjoy some music, Allah will inspire a breeze called *al-haffāfah*, which will enter the reeds of moist pipes made from pearls and stir them, causing them to hit one another. The whole of Paradise will become enraptured, and when Paradise becomes enraptured, there will not be a single tree except that it will blossom.

Abū Hurayrah ﷺ narrated that a man asked, 'O Messenger of Allah, is there any music in Paradise, for I love music?' He replied:

> Yes, by the one to whom my soul belongs. Allah will inspire the trees of Paradise to entertain His servants who engaged themselves in His remembrance at the expense of listening to musical instruments. They will produce sounds of glorification and sanctification that no creature has ever heard the like of before.

The Prophet ﷺ declared:

> There is no servant who enters Paradise save that two large-eyed maidens, one at his head and one at his feet, will sit and sing for him

---

سماع أهل الجنة، وغناء الحور العين

قال الله تعالى: ﴿وَيَوْمَ تَقُومُ ٱلسَّاعَةُ يَوْمَئِذٍ يَتَفَرَّقُونَ ۝ فَأَمَّا ٱلَّذِينَ ءَامَنُواْ وَعَمِلُواْ ٱلصَّٰلِحَٰتِ فَهُمْ فِى رَوْضَةٍ يُحْبَرُونَ ۝﴾.

قال الأوزاعي في قوله تعالى: ﴿فِى رَوْضَةٍ يُحْبَرُونَ﴾

قال: (هو السماع، وإذا أراد أهل الجنة أن يطربوا.. أوحى الله إلى رياح يقال لها: الهفافة، فدخلت في آجام قصب اللؤلؤ الرطب فحركته، فضرب بعضه بعضا، فتطرب الجنة، فإذا طربت.. لم يبق في الجنة شجرة إلا ورّدت).

وعن أبي هريرة قال: قال رجل: يا رسول الله؛ هل في الجنة سماع؛ فإني أحب السماع؟

قال: «نعم، والذي نفسي بيده، إن الله ليوحي إلى شجر الجنة أن أسمعي عبادي الذين شغلوا أنفسهم عن المعازف والمزامير بذكري، فتسمعهم بأصوات ما سمع الخلائق بمثلها قط؛ بالتسبيح والتقديس».

قال النبي ﷺ: «ما من عبد يدخل الجنة.. إلا ويجلس عند رأسه وعند رجليه ثنتان من الحور العين تغنيان بأحسن صوت سمعه الإنس والجن، وليس بمزمار الشيطان، ولكن بتمجيد الله و تقديسه».

with the most beautiful voice that any human or jinn has ever heard. They will not sing with the wood-wind instruments of the devil, but instead they will sing the praises and glory of Allah.

He ﷺ also said:

The spouses of the inhabitants of Paradise will sing for their partners with the most beautiful voices that anyone has ever heard. They will sing verses such as 'We are beautiful pleasant ones, the spouses of noble men, who look with pleasant eyes,' as well as, 'We are the eternal ones who will never die. We are the safe ones who will never fear. We are the permanent ones who will never leave.'

The Messenger of Allah ﷺ said:

The large-eyed maidens will come together in Paradise and raise their voices, the likes of which have never been heard, and sing, 'We are the eternal ones that will never perish. We are the content ones that will never be angered. We are the comfortable ones that will never be miserable. We are the permanent ones that will never leave. Glad tidings to those who belong to us and we belong to!'

Regarding the statement of the Exalted ﷻ 'And he will indeed have a status of closeness to Us and an honourable destination!',[58] Mālik ibn Dīnār ؓ said:

On the Day of Resurrection, a high pulpit will be called for and placed in Paradise. Then a call will be made: 'O Dāwūd, glorify Me with the same beautiful, melodious voice you used to glorify Me with in the temporal world.' Dawud's voice will exhaust the blessings of the inhabitants of Paradise. That is what is referred in the verse 'And he will indeed have a status of closeness to Us and an honourable destination!'

---

58 *Ṣād*, 40.

وقال:

«إن أزواج أهل الجنة ليغنّين أزواجهن بأحسن أصوات ما سمعها أحد قط، إن مما يغنين به: نحن الخيرات الحسان، أزواج قوم كرام، ينظرن بقرة أعيان، وإن مما يغنين به: نحن الخالدات فلا نموت، نحن الآمنات فلا نخاف، نحن المقيمات فلا نظعن».

وقال رسول الله ﷺ:

«إن في الجنة لمجتمعا من الحور العين، يرفعن بأصوات لم يسمع الخلائق بمثلها؛ يقلن: نحن الخالدات فلا نبيد، ونحن الناعمات فلا نبأس، ونحن الراضيات فلا نسخط، طوبى لمن كان لنا وكنا له».

قال مالك بن دينار في قوله تعالى:

﴿وَإِنَّ لَهُۥ عِندَنَا لَزُلۡفَىٰ وَحُسۡنَ مَـَٔابٍ﴾:

(إذا كان يوم القيامة.. أُمر بمنبر رفيع فوضع في الجنة، ثم نودي: يا داود؛ مجدني بذلك الصوت الحسن الرخيم الذي كنت تمجدني به في دار الدنيا، قال: فيستفرغ صوت داوود نعيم أهل الجنان، فذلك قوله: ﴿وَإِنَّ لَهُۥ عِندَنَا لَزُلۡفَىٰ وَحُسۡنَ مَـَٔابٍ﴾).

Shahr ibn Ḥawshab 🙏 narrated that the Prophet ﷺ said:

Allah will say to His Angels, 'My servants loved listening to beautiful sounds in the temporal world, but refrained from doing so for My sake. Now, let them listen!' The Angels will then sing, proclaiming the Oneness of God, glorifying Him, and exalting Him with voices the likes of which none had previously heard before.

He continued:

There is an audition greater than this, however. All types of audition are rendered obsolete in the face of this particular audition. That is when they hear the speech of their Lord. They will listen to Him addressing them with His greetings of *salām* and His noble Speech, which He Himself will read for them. When they hear it from Him, it will be as if they had never previously heard it.

'Abdullāh ibn Buraydah 🙏 narrated that the Prophet ﷺ said:

The inhabitants of Paradise will enter the presence of the Almighty (*al-Jabbār*) twice a day. He will recite the Qur'an for them while every single one of them is seated on pulpits of pearls, sapphire, chrysolite, gold, and emeralds. None of them will have ever previously been delighted by nor heard anything greater or more beautiful than it. They will then return to their homes delighted until they experience the same event the following day.

عن شهر بن حوشب قال: (إن الله جل ثناؤه يقول لملائكته:

إن عبادي كانوا يحبون الصوت الحسن في الدنيا فيدعونه من أجلي، فأسمعوا عبادي، فيأخذوا بأصوات؛ من تهليل، وتسبيح، وتكبير، لم يسمعوا بمثله قط) انتهى.

ثم قال: (ولهم سماع أعلى من هذا، يضمحل دونه كل سماع؛ وذلك حين يسمعون كلام الرب جَلَّ جَلَالُهُ، وخطابه وسلامه عليهم، ومحاضراته لهم، ويقرأ عليهم كلامه، فإذا سمعوه منه.. فكأنهم لم يسمعوه قبل ذلك).

عن عبد الله بن بريدة قال: (إن أهل الجنة يدخلون كل يوم مرتين على الجبار جَلَّ جَلَالُهُ، فيقرأ عليهم القرآن، وقد جلس كل امرىء منهم مجلسه الذي هو مجلسه على منابر الدر والياقوت والزبرجد والذهب والزمرد، فلم تقرّ أعينهم بشيء ولم يسمعوا شيئا قط أعظم ولا أحسن منه، ثم ينصرفون إلى رحالهم ناعمين، قريرة أعينهم إلى مثلها من الغد).

The Bliss of the Inhabitants of Paradise

Allah ﷻ stated, 'And if you looked around, you would see indescribable bliss and a vast kingdom.'[59] There are many manifestations of the kingdom and bliss alluded to in this verse. One of them will come in the form of the special horses provided to the inhabitants of Paradise by Allah ﷻ, which they will ride on in great processions.

Ḥasan al-Baṣrī ؓ related that the Messenger ﷺ once said:

The lowest of the inhabitants of Paradise will ride in a procession comprised of a million servants of eternal youths. They will ride on horses made of red rubies, with wings made of gold – 'And if you looked around, you would see indescribable bliss and a vast kingdom!'

'Abd al-Raḥmān ibn Sā'idah ؓ relates:

I had a love for horses, so I asked the Messenger of Allah if there would be any horses in Paradise. He replied, 'Dear 'Abd al-Raḥmān, if Allah admits you into Paradise, you will have a horse made of emeralds with two wings that will take you wherever you wish to go.'

The Prophet ﷺ said:

One of the forms of bliss that the inhabitants of Paradise will enjoy is that they will visit one another on high-bred mounts. On Fridays, they will be given saddled and bridled horses to ride, which neither defecate nor urinate, taking them wherever Allah wishes them to go.

---

59 *al-Insān*, 20.

نعيم أهل الجنة

قال الله تعالى: ﴿وَإِذَا رَأَيْتَ ثَمَّ رَأَيْتَ نَعِيمًا وَمُلْكًا كَبِيرًا﴾.

وصور هذا الملك والنعيم متعددة؛ فمنها: أن الله سبحانه وتعالى جعل لهم خيلا مخصوصة، يركبونها في مواكب كبيرة عظيمة.

عن الحسن البصري: أن الرسول ﷺ قال: «إن أدنى أهل الجنة منزلة: الذي يركب في ألف ألف من خدمه من الولدان المخلدين على خيل من ياقوت أحمر، لها أجنحة من ذهب»: ﴿وَإِذَا رَأَيْتَ ثَمَّ رَأَيْتَ نَعِيمًا وَمُلْكًا كَبِيرًا﴾.

عن عبد الرحمن بن ساعدة قال: كنت أحب الخيل، فقلت: يا رسول الله؛ هل في الجنة خيل؟ فقال: «يا عبد الرحمن؛ إن أدخلك الله الجنة.. كان لك فيها فرس من ياقوت، له جناحان يطير بك حيث شئت».

وقال ﷺ: «من نعيم أهل الجنة: أنهم يتزاورون على المطايا والنجب، وأنهم يؤتون يوم الجمعة بخيل مسرجة ملجمة، لا تروث ولا تبول، فيركبونها حتى ينتهوا حيث شاء الله تعالى».

The Prophet ﷺ also said:

There is a tree in Paradise from whose canopy garments are produced. From its trunk, saddled and bridled horses made of gold, pearls, and emeralds ride out. They neither defecate nor urinate. They are winged, and each stride they take is as far as the eye can see. When the inhabitants of Paradise mount them they will fly them to any place they wish to go. Those below them will say, 'Dear Lord, how did Your servants reach this level of honour?' They will be told, 'They would stand in prayer during the night while you were asleep. They would fast while you ate. They would spend while you were miserly. They would fight while you were cowardly.'

Another form of bliss that the inhabitants of Paradise will experience is the Divine Speech being addressed to them as follows:

'Dear inhabitants of Paradise!', Allah ﷻ will proclaim.

'At your service and aid,' they will respond.

'Are you content?' He ﷻ will ask.

'How can we not be content when You have given us that which You have never given anybody else in all of Your creation?', they will reply.

'I will give you something better than that,' He ﷻ will say.

'What is better than that?', they will ask.

He ﷻ will reply, 'I will bestow My contentment upon you, and will never be displeased with you ever again.'

Abū Hurayrah ؓ related that the Prophet ﷺ said:

A caller will proclaim: 'You shall have good health and never fall sick; you shall have life and never die; you shall have youth and never grow old; you shall have pleasure and never feel discomfort!' That

وقال ﷺ: «إن في الجنة لشجرة يخرج من أعلاها حلل، ومن أسفلها خيل من ذهب مسرجة ملجمة من درّ وياقوت، لا تروث ولا تبول، لها أجنحة، خطوها مد البصر، فيركبها أهل الجنة فتطير بهم حيث شاؤوا، فيقول الذين أسفل منهم درجة: يا رب؛ بم بلغ عبادك هذه الكرامة كلها؟ فيقال لهم: كانوا يصلون بالليل وكنتم تنامون، وكانوا يصومون وكنتم تأكلون، وكانوا ينفقون وكنتم تبخلون، وكانوا يقاتلون وكنتم تجبنون.

ومن نعيم أهل الجنّة:

ذلك النداء الرباني الذي يقول:

«يا أهل الجنة، فيقولون: لبيك ربنا وسعديك، فيقول: هل رضيتم؟ فيقولون: وما لنا لا نرضى وقد أعطيتنا ما لم تعط أحدا من خلقك؟! فيقول: أنا أعطيكم أفضل من ذلك، فيقولون: وما أفضل من ذلك؟ فيقول: أحل لكم رضواني فلا أسخط عليكم بعده أبدا».

عن أبي هريرة، عن النبي ﷺ قال:

«ينادي مناد: إن لكم أن تصحوا فلا تسقموا أبدا، وإن لكم أن تحيوا فلا تموتوا أبدا، وإن لكم أن تشبوا فلا تهرموا أبدا، وإن لكم أن تنعموا فلا تبأسوا أبدا، فذلك قوله عز وجل: ﴿وَنُودُوٓاْ أَن تِلۡكُمُ ٱلۡجَنَّةُ أُورِثۡتُمُوهَا بِمَا كُنتُمۡ تَعۡمَلُونَ﴾.

is what is meant when Allah said, 'It will be announced to them, "This is Paradise awarded to you for what you used to do."'[60]

'Alī ibn Abī Ṭālib ﷺ related that the Prophet ﷺ said:

Those who possessed consciousness of Allah (*taqwā*) will be led to Paradise in groups. When they arrive at one of its gates, they will find a tree with two streams flowing from its trunk. They will approach one of the streams. When they drink from it, all harm, impurity, and ailment will be removed from their stomachs. They will then approach the other stream and purify themselves with its water, which will cause the glow of delight (*naḍrah al-naʿīm*) to flow through them, which will cause their skin to never change again and their hair to never become dishevelled, as if it was perpetually conditioned with oil.

They will then arrive by the gatekeepers of Paradise who will say, 'Peace be upon you! You have done well, so come in, to stay forever.'[61]

They will then be received by eternal youths, who will move around them, just as people in the temporal world do when they meet an intimate friend after an absence, and say, 'Rejoice at the honouring that Allah has prepared for you!'

Then one of the eternal youths will go to one of the believer's spouses from among the large-eyed maidens and say, 'So-and-so' – using the name that he was known by in the temporal world – 'has just arrived.' 'Have you seen him?' she will ask, to which he will reply, 'Yes, I have seen him. He is not far behind!' This will make her so excited that she will rush to receive him at her doorstep. When the believer reaches his home, he will look to see what the foundations of his house are made of and will behold a mass of pearls upon which a structure of green, yellow, red, and every colour imaginable is built. He will then raise his head and look at the ceiling, which will emit a light that resembles lightning. Had Allah not decreed it for him, it

---

60 *al-Aʿrāf*, 43.

61 *al-Zumar*, 73.

وعن علي بن أبي طالب ﵁ قال

: (يساق الذين اتقوا ربهم إلى الجنة زمرا، حتى إذا انتهوا إلى باب من أبوابها.. وجدوا عنده شجرة يخرج من تحت ساقها عينان تجريان، فعمدوا إلى إحداهما؛ كأنما أمروا بها، فشربوا منها، فذهب ما في بطونهم من أذى أو قذى أو بأس، ثمّ عمدوا إلى الأخرى فتطهروا منها، فجرت عليهم نضرة النعيم، فلن تتغير أبشارهم بعدها أبدا، و لن تشعث أشعارهم؛ كأنما دهنوا بالدهان.

ثم انتهوا إلى خزنة الجنة فقالوا: ﴿سَلَٰمٌ عَلَيۡكُمۡ طِبۡتُمۡ فَٱدۡخُلُوهَا خَٰلِدِينَ﴾.

ثم تلقاهم الولدان يطوفون بهم كما يطوف أهل الدنيا بالحميم يقدم من غيبته، فيقولون: أبشر بما أعد الله لك من الكرامة.

ثم ينطلق غلام من أولئك الولدان إلى بعض أزواجه من الحور العين فيقول: قد جاء فلان - باسمه الذي كان يدعى به في الدنيا - فتقول: أنت رأيته؟ فيقول: أنا رأيته، وهو ذا بأثري، فيستخف إحداهن الفرح حتى تقوم على أسكفه بابها، فإذا انتهى إلى منزله.. نظر إلى أي شيء أساس بنيانه، فإذا جندل اللؤلؤ، فوقه صرح أخضر وأصفر وأحمر، ومن كل لون، ثم رفع رأسه فنظر إلى سقفه، فإذا مثل البرق، لولا أن الله قدره له لألم أن يذهب ببصره، ثم طأطأ رأسه فنظر إلى أزواجه، وأكواب موضوعة، ونمارق مصفوفة، وزرابي مبثوثة.

would have blinded him. He will look back down and see his spouses, cups set at hand, fine cushions lined up, and splendid carpets spread out.

They will see all these blessings and recite, 'And they will say, "Praise be to Allah for guiding us to this. We would never have been guided if Allah had not guided us."'[62] Then a caller will proclaim, 'You will live forever and never die! You will live here permanently and never leave! You will be healthy and never be sick again!'

---

62   *al-Aʿrāf*, 43.

فنظروا إلى تلك النعمة ثم تلوا: ﴿وَقَالُوا۟ ٱلْحَمْدُ لِلَّهِ ٱلَّذِى هَدَىٰنَا لِهَٰذَا وَمَا كُنَّا لِنَهْتَدِىَ لَوْلَآ أَنْ هَدَىٰنَا ٱللَّهُ﴾.

ثم ينادي مناد: تحيون فلا تموتون أبدا، وتقيمون فلا تظعنون أبدا، وتصحون فلا تمرضون أبدا).

The Inhabitants of Paradise & Their States

The Prophet ﷺ once said, 'It is my hope that those of my Ummah who follow me will comprise a quarter of the inhabitants of Paradise on the Day of Resurrection.' The narrator of the Hadith then added, 'We said "God is Great" (*Allāhu Akbar*).' He continued, 'It is my hope that you make up a third of the people.' We said, 'God is Great.' He then said, 'It is my hope that you make up half of them.'

The inhabitants of Paradise will make up one hundred and twenty rows, eighty of which will be composed of this Ummah while the other forty will be made up of all the other Ummahs put together.

As for the inhabitants of Paradise, the Prophet ﷺ has informed us that there will be some people who enter Paradise whose hearts resemble the hearts of birds. Al-Qurṭubī commented:

> There are two ways to understand this statement. The first is that they resemble birds in the fear and awe that they manifest, since birds are the most fearful and cautious of animals. The second is that they are similar to them in softness and fragility. The people of Yemen are described as being 'the most gentle-hearted and soft-hearted of people.' There is also a third possibility, which is that they are free of all sin and faults, oblivious of the affairs of the temporal world.

One of the attributes of the inhabitants of Paradise is described in a Hadith in which the Prophet ﷺ said:

> Should I not tell you who the inhabitants of Paradise are? They include every weak and humbled person. If they were to take an oath that Allah will do something, He would fulfil it. Should I not tell

أهل الجنة وأحوالهم

قال ﷺ: «إني لأرجو أن يكون من يتبعني من أمتي يوم القيامة ربع أهل الجنة» فكبرنا، ثم قال: «أرجو أن تكونوا ثلث الناس» فكبرنا، ثم قال: «إني أرجو أن تكونوا الشطر».

وأهل الجنة عشرون ومئة صف، ثمانون منها من هذه الأمة، وأربعون من سائر الأمم.

أهل الجنة

أما أهل الجنة.. فقد أخبرنا ﷺ أنه يدخل الجنة أقوام أفئدتهم مثل أفئدة الطير، قال القرطبي: (في تأويله وجهان:

أحدهما: أنها مثلها في الخوف والهيبة، والطير أكثر الحيوانات خوفا وحذرا.

والثاني: أنها مثلها في الضعف والرقة، كما جاء في وصف أهل اليمن: «أرق قلوبا، وأضعف أفئدة».

ويحتمل وجها ثالثا: أنها مثلها في أنها خالية من كل ذنب، سليمة من كل عيب،

you who the inhabitants of the Fire are? They include every coarse ('*utull*), haughty (*jawwāz*), and arrogant person.

Al-Qurṭubī commented that the word 'weak' means 'weak in the affairs of the temporal world, but strong in the affairs of his religion.'

'Utull is a word used to describe a harsh and argumentative person, while others contend that it is used to refer to an oppressive person who eats and drinks excessively. Another opinion states that it means someone who is rude and callous, and can in no way be encouraged to do good. The term *jawwāz* refers to someone who amasses wealth yet remains miserly. Others contend that it means hard-hearted, while another opinion is that it refers to a fleshy and haughty person.

Another attribute of the inhabitants of Paradise has been described in a Hadith by the Messenger of Allah ﷺ as follows:

> The first group to enter Paradise will take the form of the full moon. The group that follows them will resemble the most brilliantly shining star. They will neither urinate nor defecate, nor will they emit saliva or mucus. Their combs will be of gold; their sweat will be like musk; their incense burners will be of Indian agarwood (*aluwwah*). The large-eyed maidens will be their spouses. Their character will be like that of a single man upon the form of their father Adam reaching sixty cubits high.

He ﷺ also said:

> The inhabitants of Paradise will enter Paradise beardless and without bodily hair, fair-skinned, with compact and strong bodies and kohl in their eyes. They will be thirty-three years of age and of the same stature as Adam, measuring sixty cubits tall and seven cubits wide.

لا خبرة لهم بأمور الدنيا.

و من صفات أهل الجنة:

ما جاء في الحديث: أن النبي ﷺ قال: «ألا أخبركم بأهل الجنة؟ كل ضعيف متضعف، لو أقسم على الله.. لأبره، ألا أخبركم بأهل النار؟ كلُّ عُتُل جواظ مستكبر».

قال القرطبي: (يعني: ضعيفا في أمور الدنيا، قويا في أمور دينه).

و(**العتل**): الجافي الشديد الخصومة، وقيل: الأكول الشروب الظلوم، وقيل: الفظ الغليظ، الذي لا ينقاد لخير.

و(**الجواظ**): الجموع المنوع، وقيل: الجافي القلب، وقيل: الكثير اللحم المختال.

ومن صفات أهل الجنة: ما جاء في الحديث عن رسول الله ﷺ قال: «أول زمرة تدخل الجنة على صورة القمر ليلة البدر، والذين يلونهم على أشد كوكب درّي في السماء إضاءة، لا يبولون ولا يتغوطون، ولا يتفلون ولا يمتخطون، أمشاطهم الذهب، ورشحهم المسك، ومجامرهم الألوة، وأزواجهم الحور العين، أخلاقهم على خلق رجل واحد، على صورة أبيهم آدم؛ ستون ذراعا في السماء».

وقال: «يدخل أهل الجنة الجنة جردا مردا، بيضا جعادا، مكحَّلين، أبناء ثلاث

The inhabitants of Paradise will speak in Arabic, and will have fair faces, such that none of them will be dark-skinned. Allah ﷻ has informed us that they will visit one another in Paradise:

> They will turn to one another inquisitively. They will say, 'Before [this reward] we used to be in awe of Allah in the midst of our people. So Allah has graced us and protected us from the torments of Hell's scorching heat. Indeed we used to call upon Him alone aforetime. He is truly the Most Kind, Most Merciful.'[63]

The Prophet ﷺ explained what this means, saying:

> After the inhabitants of Paradise have entered Paradise, they will yearn for their brothers. Their couches will be brought together and they will recline on them. They will then speak about life in the temporal world. One of them will say to his friend, 'Do you know on what day Allah forgave us?' to which his friend will reply, 'On the day we were in such-and-such a place. We prayed to Allah and He forgave us.'

The Prophet ﷺ also said, 'The Inhabitants of Paradise will visit one another on white, high-bred mounts that resemble sapphires.' Allah ﷻ has declared:

> Then they will turn to one another inquisitively. One of them will say, 'I once had a companion in the world who used to ask me, "Do you actually believe in the Resurrection? When we are dead and reduced to dust and bones, will we really be brought to judgment?"' He will then ask, 'Would you care to see his fate?' Then he and the others will look and spot him in the midst of the Hellfire. He will then say, 'By Allah! You nearly ruined me. Had it not been for the

---

63 *al-Ṭūr*, 25-28.

وثلاثين، وهم على خلق آدم، طوله ستون ذراعا، في عرض سبعة أذرع».

وأهل الجنة يتكلمون باللغة العربية.

وكلهم بيض الوجوه، ليس فيهم أسود.

وهم في الجنة يتزاورون كما قال الله تعالى: ﴿وَأَقۡبَلَ بَعۡضُهُمۡ عَلَىٰ بَعۡضٖ يَتَسَآءَلُونَ ٢٥ قَالُوٓاْ إِنَّا كُنَّا قَبۡلُ فِيٓ أَهۡلِنَا مُشۡفِقِينَ ٢٦ فَمَنَّ ٱللَّهُ عَلَيۡنَا وَوَقَىٰنَا عَذَابَ ٱلسَّمُومِ ٢٧ إِنَّا كُنَّا مِن قَبۡلُ نَدۡعُوهُۖ إِنَّهُۥ هُوَ ٱلۡبَرُّ ٱلرَّحِيمُ ٢٨﴾.

ويبين ذلك ﷺ بقوله: «إذا دخل أهل الجنة الجنة.. اشتاقوا إلى الإخوان، فيجيء سرير هذا حتى يحاذي سرير هذا، فيتكئ هذا ويتكئ هذا، ويتحدثان بما كان في الدنيا.

فيقول أحدهما لصاحبه: يا فلان؛ تدري يوم غفر الله لنا؟ فيقول صاحبه: يوم كنا في موضع كذا وكذا، فدعونا الله فغفر لنا».

وقال ﷺ: «إن أهل الجنة يتزاورون على نجائب بيض كأنهن الياقوت».

وقال تعالى: ﴿فَأَقۡبَلَ بَعۡضُهُمۡ عَلَىٰ بَعۡضٖ يَتَسَآءَلُونَ ٥٠ قَالَ قَآئِلٞ مِّنۡهُمۡ إِنِّي كَانَ لِي قَرِينٞ ٥١ يَقُولُ أَءِنَّكَ لَمِنَ ٱلۡمُصَدِّقِينَ ٥٢ أَءِذَا مِتۡنَا وَكُنَّا تُرَابٗا وَعِظَٰمًا أَءِنَّا لَمَدِينُونَ ٥٣ قَالَ هَلۡ أَنتُم مُّطَّلِعُونَ ٥٤ فَٱطَّلَعَ فَرَءَاهُ فِي سَوَآءِ

grace of my Lord, I too would have certainly been among those brought to Hell!'[64]

Allah ﷻ has informed us that the inhabitants of Paradise will turn to one another to talk. They will talk about how things used to be in the temporal world. Their discussion will lead on to one of them saying, 'I once had a companion in the temporal world who did not believe in the Resurrection and Hereafter. He would say what Allah ﷻ has quoted – 'Do you actually believe in the Resurrection?' – and would ask if we really would be resurrected, rewarded for our actions, and be held to account even after our bodies have decomposed and we have turned to dust and bones. This believer will then ask his brothers in Paradise, 'Are you able to look into the Fire so that we may see what happened to that companion of mine?'

He will then be able to see his companion in the depths of hell. Were it not for the fact that Allah ﷻ had told him who it was, he would not have recognised him for his face and colour had changed, as the punishment had left him unrecognisable. At this point he will say, 'By Allah! You nearly ruined me. Had it not been for the grace of my Lord, I too would have certainly been amongst those brought to Hell!' – meaning that his companion nearly destroyed him. Had it not been for the grace that the Lord ﷻ bestowed upon him, he would have been with his companion amongst those who were cast into the Eternal Punishment of Allah ﷻ.

The Messenger of Allah ﷺ was asked, 'Will the inhabitants of Paradise visit one another?' He replied, 'The inhabitants of the higher levels will visit the inhabitants of the lower levels. However, the inhabitants of the lower levels cannot visit the higher levels, except

---

64 *al-Ṣāffāt*, 50-57.

ٱلْجَحِيمِ ۝ قَالَ تَٱللَّهِ إِن كِدتَّ لَتُرْدِينِ ۝ وَلَوْلَا نِعْمَةُ رَبِّي لَكُنتُ مِنَ ٱلْمُحْضَرِينَ ۝.

أخبر سبحانه أن أهل الجنة أقبل بعضهم على بعض يتحدثون، ويسأل بعضهم بعضا عن أحوال كانت في الدنيا، فأفضت بهم المحادثة والمذاكرة إلى أن قال قائل منهم: إني كان لي قرين في الدنيا ينكر البعث والدار الآخرة، ويقول ما حكاه الله بقوله: ﴿أَءِنَّكَ لَمِنَ ٱلْمُصَدِّقِينَ﴾ بأنا نبعث ونجازى بأعمالنا، ونحاسب بها بعد أن مزقنا البلى، وكنا ترابا وعظاما؟!

ثم يقول المؤمن لإخوانه في الجنة: هل أنتم مطلعون في النار؛ لننظر منزلة قريني هذا وما صار إليه؟

فأشرف فرأى قرينه في وسط الجحيم، ولولا أن الله عرفه إياه.. لما عرفه؛ لقد تغير وجهه ولونه، وغيره العذاب أشد تغيير،

فعندها قال الله تعالى: ﴿تَٱللَّهِ إِن كِدتَّ لَتُرْدِينِ ۝ وَلَوْلَا نِعْمَةُ رَبِّي لَكُنتُ مِنَ ٱلْمُحْضَرِينَ ۝﴾؛

أي: إن كدت لتهلكني، ولولا أن أنعم الله علي بنعمته.. لكنت من المحضرين معك في العذاب.

for those who loved one another for the sake of Allah. They will be able to come from wherever they are on camels.'

In summary, the inhabitants of Paradise will be able to visit one another and ask each other about things, which will complete their pleasure and happiness. The Prophet ﷺ once asked Ḥārithah ؓ, 'How are you this morning, Ḥārithah?' He replied, 'A true believer.' The Prophet ﷺ responded, 'Everything has a reality. What is the reality of your belief?' He replied, 'My lower self has shunned the temporal world. I keep awake in prayer during the night and I make myself thirsty by fasting during the day. My belief is so strong that it is as though I can actually witness the Throne of my Lord before me, watch the inhabitants of Paradise visiting one another, and behold the inhabitants of the Fire being punished.' The Prophet ﷺ said, 'You are a servant whose heart Allah has illuminated.'

وقد سئل رسول الله ﷺ: أيتزاور أهل الجنة؟ قال: «يزور الأعلى الأسفل، ولا يزور الأسفل الأعلى، إلا الذين يتحابون في الله يأتون منها حيث شاؤوا على النوق».

فأهل الجنة يتزاورون فيها، ويسأل بعضهم بعضا، وبذلك تتم لذتهم وسرورهم، ولهذا قال حارثة للنبي ﷺ وقد سأله: «كيف أصبحت يا حارثة؟» قال: أصبحت مؤمنا حقا، قال: «إن لكل حق حقيقة، فما حقيقة إيمانك؟» قال: عزفت نفسي عن الدنيا، فأسهرت ليلي، وأظمأت نهاري، وكأني أنظر إلى عرش ربي بارزا، وإلى أهل الجنة يتزاورون فيها، وإلى أهل النار يعذبون فيها، فقال: «عبد نور الله قلبه».

The Inhabitants of Paradise Visit their Lord

The theophany has been alluded to in the verse in which Allah ﷻ states 'on that Day some faces will be bright, looking at their Lord.'[65] Regarding this, the Prophet ﷺ said:

When the inhabitants of Paradise enter Paradise, Allah will say, 'Do you want Me to give you more?' They will reply, 'Have You not illuminated our faces? Have You not admitted us to Paradise and saved us from the Fire?' The veil will then be lifted and there will nothing more pleasing to them than beholding their Lord. 'Those who do good will have the finest reward and even more.'[66]

He ﷺ also said:

On the Day of Resurrection, Allah will send a summoner who will proclaim with a voice that the first and last of them will all hear, crying out 'O inhabitants of Paradise! Allah has indeed promised you the finest reward and even more! Paradise is the finest reward; this 'more' is beholding the Countenance of the Most Merciful.'

It has also been narrated that the inhabitants of Paradise will visit their Lord every Friday. During that visit, Allah ﷻ will say, 'I am the One Who fulfilled My promise to you and completed My favour upon you. This is where My Generosity resides, so ask of Me.' They will ask Him ﷻ for His contentment with them, to which He ﷻ will say, 'My contentment is what has brought you to My abode and

---

65 *al-Qiyāmah*, 22-23.
66 *Yūnus*, 26.

زيارة أهل الجنة ربهم

وهذا ما اشار إليه الله تعالى بقوله: ﴿وُجُوهٌ يَوْمَئِذٍ نَّاضِرَةٌ ۝ إِلَىٰ رَبِّهَا نَاظِرَةٌ ۝﴾.

قال ﷺ: «إذا دخل أهل الجنة الجنة.. يقول الله تبارك وتعالى: تريدون شيئا أزيدكم؟ فيقولون: ألم تبيض وجوهنا؟! ألم تدخلنا الجنة وتنجنا من النار؟!

قال: فيكشف الحجاب، فما أعطوا شيئا أحب إليهم من النظر إلى ربهم»، ثم تلا هذه الآية: ﴿لِّلَّذِينَ أَحْسَنُوا۟ الْحُسْنَىٰ وَزِيَادَةٌ﴾.

وقال: «إن الله يبعث يوم القيامة مناديا ينادي بصوت يسمعه أولهم وآخرهم: يا أهل الجنة، إن الله وعدكم الحسنى وزيادة؛ فالحسنى: الجنة، والزيادة: النظر إلى وجه الرحمن».

وجاء أن أهل الجنة يزورون ربهم يوم الجمعة، فيقول الله تعالى لهم في تلك الزيارة: «أنا الذي صدقتكم وعدي، وأتممت عليكم نعمتي، هذا محل كرامتي فاسألوني، فيسألون الرضا، فيقول عزوجل: رضائي أحلكم داري، وأنالكم كرامتي، فاسألوني، فيسألونه حتى تنتهي رغبتهم».

enabled you to receive My generosity, so ask of Me.' They will then continue to ask of Him until their desires are fulfilled.

At this point He, will avail them of that which no eye has ever seen, no ear has ever heard, and no human heart has ever imagined. This will continue until all the people visiting on Friday have departed. They will not yearn for anything as they will yearn for Friday. For on that day, they will be honoured more than usual and will gaze upon His Countenance. It is for this reason that Friday is called the Day of Increase.

'Alī ﷺ has narrated that:

The Prophet ﷺ said, 'When the inhabitants of Paradise have settled in Paradise, an Angel will come to them and say, 'Allah has commanded you to visit Him.' When they have assembled, Allah will command Dāwūd ﷺ, who will raise his voice singing the Glory and Oneness of Allah. Thereafter, the Banquet of Eternity will be spread.'

The Companions then asked, 'O Messenger of Allah, what is the Banquet of Eternity?' He replied, 'A single one of its corners is more vast than what lies between the east and the west. They will eat, drink and be clothed in robes of honour. Then they will say, "Nothing remains but for us to look upon the Countenance of our Lord." He will then reveal Himself to them, and they will fall down in prostration. At this they will be told, "You are not in the Abode of Deeds; rather, you are in the Abode of Reward."'

Another narration informs us that the inhabitants of Paradise will have a gathering with Allah ﷻ in which He will address every single one of them. The Prophet ﷺ said:

There will not be a single man in that gathering except that Allah will speak to him individually, to the extent that He will say to one of them, 'O So-and-so, do you remember the day you did such-and-such a thing?' He will remind him of some of the wrongs that he had committed in the temporal world. The man will say, 'My Lord, have

فيفتح لهم عند ذلك ما لا عين رأت، ولا أذن سمعت، ولا خطر على بال قلب بشر، إلى مقدار منصرف الناس يوم الجمعة.

فليسوا إلى شيء أحوج منهم إلى يوم الجمعة؛ ليزدادوا فيه كرامة، وليزدادوا فيه نظرا إلى وجهه تبارك وتعالى، ولذلك دعي يوم المزيد».

عن علي قال: إذا سكن أهل الجنة الجنة.. أتاهم ملك فيقول: إن الله أمركم أن تزوروه، فيجتمعون، فيأمر الله داوود عليه السلام فيرفع صوته بالتسبيح والتهليل، ثم توضع مائدة الخلد.

قالوا: يا رسول الله؛ وما مائدة الخلد؟ قال: «زاوية من زواياها أوسع مما بين المشرق والمغرب، فيطعمون، ثم يُسقون، ثم يُكسون، فيقولون: لم يبق لنا إلا النظر إلى وجه ربنا عز وجل.

فيتجلى لهم، فيخرون سجدا، فيقال لهم: لستم في دار عمل، إنما أنتم في دار جزاء».

وجاء في الآثار: أن لأهل الجنة مع الله مجلسا يخاطب فيه كل واحد منهم، قال ﷺ: «حتى لا يبقى في ذلك المجلس رجل إلا حاضره الله محاضرة، حتى يقول للرجل منهم: يا فلان بن فلان؛ أتذكر يوم فعلت كذا وكذا؟! فيذكره ببعض غدراته في الدنيا، فيقول: يا ربّ؛ أفلم تغفر لي؟ فيقول: بلى؛ بسعة مغفرتي بلغت منزلتك هذه..

You not forgiven me?' He will reply, 'Indeed! It is only because of My Forgiveness that you have reached the station you are in.'

While this is going on, a cloud will form above them and rain down a perfume that none had previously smelt anything like it. Our Lord will say, 'Go forth and enjoy the honour I have prepared for you, and take whatever you desire!'

فبينما هم على ذلك.. غشيتهم سحابة من فوقهم، فأمطرت عليهم طيبا لم يجدوا مثل ريحه شيئا قط، يقول ربنا: قوموا إلى ما أعددت لكم من الكرامة، فخذوا ما اشتهيتم».

The Market of Paradise

Sa'īd ibn al-Musayyib ﷺ relayed that he once met Abū Hurayrah ﷺ who said, 'I ask Allah to bring us together in the market of Paradise.' Sa'īd ﷺ then asked, 'Is there a market there?' He ﷺ replied, 'Yes. The Messenger of Allah ﷺ informed me', and then he narrated the following Hadith:

> After visiting the Real ﷻ in Paradise, they will go to a marketplace, which will be surrounded by Angels. In it will be things the likes of which eyes have never seen, ears have never heard, and hearts have never imagined. Whatever we desire will be carried for us. There will be no buying or selling.
>
> In that marketplace, the inhabitants of Paradise will meet one another. When a man of high status meets someone of a lower status – though there is no one of low status there – the latter will be impressed by the clothing of his friend. By the time their conversation has ended, he will be presented with a garment that is even finer than his friend's. This is because no one ought to feel any sadness there.
>
> They will then return to their homes, where they will be received by their spouses. They will say, 'Welcome home! You have returned more beautiful than when you had left!' Those returning will reply, 'Today we have kept the company of our Lord, the Almighty. It is only fitting that we return in the state that we have."

One of the Salaf ﷺ said:

> The days of celebration (Eid) for the believers in Paradise will be the days they visit their Lord. When they visit Him, He will honour them in the most sublime manner. He will reveal Himself to them,

سوق الجنة

عن سعيد بن المسيب: أنه لقي أبا هريرة، فقال أبو هريرة: (أسأل الله أن يجمع بيني وبينك في سوق الجنة)، فقال سعيد: أفيها سوق؟ قال: (نعم، أخبرني رسول الله ﷺ...) وساق حديثا طويلا وفيه: «أنهم بعد زيارة الحق ﷻ في الجنة يأتون سوقا قد حفت به الملائكة، مما لم تنظر العيون إلى مثله، ولم تسمع الآذان، ولم يخطر على القلوب، فيحمل لنا ما اشتهينا، ليس يباع فيها ولا يشترى.

وفي ذلك السوق يلقى أهل الجنة بعضهم بعضا، فيقبل الرجل ذو المنزلة الرفيعة، فيلقى من هو دونه - وما فيهم دني - فيروعه ما يرى عليه من اللباس، فما ينقضي آخر حديثه حتى يتمثل له ما هو أحسن منه، وذلك أنه لا ينبغي لأحد أن يحزن فيها.

ثم ننصرف إلى منازلنا، فيتلقانا أزواجنا، فيقلن: مرحبا وأهلا، لقد جئت وإنّ لك من الجمال أفضل مما قد فارقتنا عليه.

فيقول: إنا جالسنا اليوم ربنا الجبار، ويحق لنا أن ننقلب بمثل ما انقلبنا».

قال بعض السلف: (أعياد المؤمنين في الجنة أيام زيارتهم لربهم ﷻ، فيزورونه، ويكرمهم غاية الكرامة، ويتجلى لهم فينظرون إليه، فما أعطاهم شيئا هو أحبّ إليهم من ذلك؛ وهو الزيادة التي قال الله فيها: ﴿لِّلَّذِينَ أَحْسَنُواْ ٱلْحُسْنَىٰ وَزِيَادَةٌ﴾،

and they will look upon Him. There is nothing that He will give them that is more beloved to them than this. This is the 'more' referred to in the verse 'Those who do good will have the finest reward and even more.'[67] Only when he is close to his beloved does a lover consider a day to be a day of celebration.

Only a day that reunites me with them –
That is Eid; I have no Eid besides that!

Every day of celebration that Muslims celebrate in the temporal world will be a day of celebration for them in Paradise. On these days, they will come together to meet their Lord, and He will reveal Himself to them. In Paradise, Friday is known as the Day of Increase. The inhabitants of Paradise will also visit one another on the days of Eid al-Fitr and Eid al-Adha. This is for the masses of the inhabitants of Paradise.

For the Elect, however, every day will be a day of celebration. They will see their Lord every day, twice a day, morning and evening. Every day in the temporal world was a day of celebration for the Elect, so every day in the Hereafter will also be a day of celebration for them.

---

67 *Yūnus*, 26.

فليس للمحبّ عيد سوى قرب محبوبه.

شعر:

إن يوما جامعا شملي بهم   *   ذاك عيد ليس لي عيد سواه

كل يوم للمسلمين عيد في الدنيا.. فإنه عيد لهم في الجنة، يجتمعون فيه على زيارة ربهم، ويتجلى لهم فيه، ويوم الجمعة يُدعىٰ في الجنة يوم المزيد، وأيام الفطر والأضحى يجتمع أهل الجنة فيها للزيارة، فهذا لعموم أهل الجنة.

فأما خواصهم.. فكل يوم لهم عيد، يرون ربهم كل يوم مرتين؛ بكرة وعشيا. الخواص كانت أيام الدنيا كلها لهم أعيادا، فصارت أيامهم في الآخرة كلها أعياداً).

The Immortality of the Inhabitants of Paradise

Allah ﷻ declares, 'And as for those destined to joy, they will be in Paradise, staying there forever, as long as the Heavens and the Earth will endure, except what your Lord wills – a generous bestowal without end.'[68]

The Prophet ﷺ stated:

> After the inhabitants of Paradise have entered Paradise and the inhabitants of the Fire have entered the Fire, an announcer (*mu'adh-dhin*) will rise and proclaim: 'O inhabitants of the Fire, there is no more death! O inhabitants of Paradise, there is no more death! All shall remain where they are in eternity!'

The Messenger of Allah ﷺ also said:

> After the inhabitants of Paradise have entered Paradise and the inhabitants of the Fire have entered the Fire, death will be brought forth and placed between Paradise and the Fire. It will then be slaughtered and an announcer will proclaim: 'O inhabitants of Paradise, there is no more death! O Inhabitants of the Fire, there is no more death!' This event will only serve to increase the joy of the inhabitants of Paradise and multiply the misery of the inhabitants of the Fire.

---

68 *Hūd*, 108.

خلود أهل الجنة

قال الله تعالى: ﴿وَأَمَّا ٱلَّذِينَ سُعِدُواْ فَفِى ٱلْجَنَّةِ خَٰلِدِينَ فِيهَا مَا دَامَتِ ٱلسَّمَٰوَٰتُ وَٱلْأَرْضُ إِلَّا مَا شَآءَ رَبُّكَ عَطَآءً غَيْرَ مَجْذُوذٍ ۝﴾.

وقال النبي ﷺ:

«يدخل أهل الجنة الجنة، وأهل النار النار، ثم يقوم مؤذن بينهم: يا أهل النار؛ لا موت، ويا أهل الجنة؛ لا موت، كل خالد فيما هو فيه».

وقال رسول الله ﷺ:

«إذا صار أهل الجنة إلى الجنة، وأهل النار إلى النار.. جيء بالموت حتى يجعل بين الجنة والنار، ثم يذبح، ثم ينادي مناد: يا أهل الجنة، لاموت، ويا أهل النار، لا موت، فيزداد أهل الجنة فرحا إلى فرحهم، ويزداد أهل النار حزنا إلى حزنهم».

The First and Last People to Enter Paradise

The first person to enter Paradise will be our Master and Lord, the Messenger of Allah, Muhammad ﷺ, the son of ʿAbdullāh. He informed us of this in his statement:

I will approach the gate of Paradise on the Day of Resurrection and will ask for it to be opened. The gatekeeper will ask who it is, to which I will reply that it is Muhammad. He will then say, 'I was ordered not to open for anyone before you.'

He ﷺ also said, 'Paradise is forbidden to the Prophets until I enter it. It is likewise forbidden to all Ummahs until my Ummah enters it.'

He ﷺ was also asked about the different orders in which people will enter Paradise. Jābir ﷺ narrated that a man asked:

'O Messenger of Allah, which people will enter Paradise first on the Day of Resurrection?'

He replied, 'The Prophets.'

'Then who?' asked the man.

'The martyrs,' he replied.

'Then who?' he inquired.

'The *muʾadhdhin*s of the Kaʿbah.'

'Then who?' he asked.

'The *muʾadhdhin*s of Jerusalem,' he replied.

'Then who?' he asked.

أول من يدخل الجنة، وآخر أهلها دخولا فيها

أول من يدخل الجنة:

هو سيدنا ومولانا رسول الله محمد بن عبد الله.

وقد بين ذلك بقوله: «آتي باب الجنة يوم القيامة، فأستفتح، فيقول الخازن: من أنت؟ فأقول: محمد، فيقول: بك أمرت ألا أفتح لأحد قبلك».

وبقوله ﷺ: «الجنة حرمت على الأنبياء حتى أدخلها، وحرمت على الأمم حتى تدخلها أمتي».

وقد سئل عن مراتب الناس في الدخول:

فعن جابر أن رجلا قال: يا رسول الله؛ أي الخلق أسبق دخولا إلى الجنة يوم القيامة؟ قال: «الأنبياء»، قال: ثم من؟ قال: «الشهداء»، قال: ثم من؟ قال: «مؤذنو الكعبة»، قال: ثم من

؟ قال: «مؤذنو بيت المقدس»، قال: ثم من؟ قال: «مؤذنو مسجدي هذا»، قال: ثم من؟ قال: «سائر المؤذنين على قدر أعمالهم».

'The *mu'adhdhins* of this mosque of mine,' he replied.

'Then who,' he asked.

'All other *mu'adhdhins* according to their deeds,' he replied.

One of the groups of people that will enter Paradise first are known as the *ḥammādūn*, those who praise Allah ﷻ in times of both weal and woe. The poor will also be amongst the first to enter. The Prophet ﷺ said:

> The poor will arrive at Paradise before other people. When they do, the Angels will come out to them and say, 'Go back to be held to account!' They will respond, 'What are to be held accountable for? By Allah, we were not blessed with wealth such that we could withhold or spend. We were not given authority such that we could be just or unjust. Rather, when the decree of Allah became known to us, we worshipped Him until death.'

Other types of people who will be amongst the first to enter Paradise include the martyrs; slaves who both worshipped their Lord and served their masters well; and modest and virtuous men.

It is narrated that the Messenger of Allah ﷺ said, 'The first three types of people to enter the Fire will be an oppressive ruler; a wealthy person who does not fulfil the rights Allah has over his wealth, and a haughty pauper.'

As for the last person to escape the Fire, the Messenger of Allah ﷺ said:

> I know of the last of the inhabitants of Fire to leave the Fire and the last of the inhabitants of Paradise to enter Paradise, a man who will leave the Fire crawling. Allah will say to him, 'Go and enter Paradise!' When he gets there, he will be given the impression that it is full and so he will return and say, 'My Lord, it was full.' Allah will say to him, 'Go and enter Paradise!' When he gets there, he will be given

ومن أول من يدخل الجنة:

الحمّادون؛ الذين يحمدون الله في السرّاء والضرّاء.

ومن أول من يدخل الجنة

: الفقراء؛ قال ﷺ: «الفقراء يسبقون الناس إلى الجنة، فيخرج إليهم منها ملائكة فيقولون: ارجعوا إلى الحساب، فيقولون: علام نحاسب؟! والله؛ ما أفيضت علينا الأموال في الدنيا فنقبض منها ونبسط، وما كنا أمراء نعدل ونجور، ولكنا جاءنا أمر الله فعبدناه حتى أتانا اليقين».

ومن أول من يدخل الجنة

: الشهيد، والعبد المملوك الذي أحسن عبادة ربه وخدمة سيده، والرجل العفيف المتعفف.

عن رسول الله ﷺ أنه قال: «وأما أول ثلاثة يدخلون النار: فأمير مسلّط، وذو ثروة من مال لا يعطي حق الله في ماله، وفقير فخور».

وأما آخر من يخرج من النار.. فقد قال رسول الله ﷺ: «إني لأعلم آخر أهل النار خروجا منها، وآخر أهل الجنة دخولا الجنة؛ رجل يخرج من النار حَبْواً، فيقول الله له: اذهب فادخل الجنة، فيأتيها، فيخيل إليه أنها ملأى، فيرجع فيقول: يا رب؛

the impression that it is full, and so he will return and say, 'My Lord, it was full.' Allah will say to him, 'Go and enter Paradise! For you will have the likes of the world ten times over.' He will say, 'Do you mock me despite being the King?'

In a similar narration the Messenger of Allah ﷺ said:

The last person to enter Paradise will be a man who will at times walk and at times stumble. The Fire will even scorch him at times. When he has finally passed it, he will turn to it and say, 'Glory be to the One who has saved me from you. Allah has given me something that He has not given anyone from the first generations, nor the last.'

A tree will then be raised for him and he will say, 'My Lord, bring me close to this tree so that I may take shade in its shadow and drink from its water.' Allah will reply, 'O Son of Adam, if I let you have that, you might ask Me for something else.' He will say, 'My Lord…' and promise Him that he will not ask for anything else. His Lord will excuse him, because He knows this man has seen something he cannot resist. Allah will then bring him close to the tree, and he will then take shade in its shadow and drink from its water.

Then another tree, superior to the first one, will be raised for him. He will say, 'My Lord, bring me close to this tree so that I may drink from its water and take shade in its shadow. I will not ask You for anything else.' Allah will say, 'Son of Adam, did you not already promise Me that you would not ask Me for anything else? If I bring you close to this one, you will ask Me for something else!'

He will then make another promise that he will not ask for anything else. His Lord will excuse him, as He knows that the man has seen something he cannot resist. Allah will then bring the man close to the tree, and he will then take shade in its shadow and drink from its water.

Then another tree, even better than the first two, will be raised for him at the gate of Paradise. He will say, 'My Lord, bring me close to this tree so that I may take shade in its shadow and drink from its water. I will not ask You for anything else.' Allah will say, 'Son of

وجدتها ملأى، فيقول الله له: اذهب فادخل الجنة، قال: فيأتيها، فيخيل إليه أنها ملأى، فيرجع فيقول: يا رب؛ وجدتها ملأى، فيقول الله له: اذهب فادخل الجنة؛ فإن لك مثل الدنيا وعشرة أمثالها، فيقول: أتسخر بي وأنت الملك؟!».

وفي رواية: أن رسول الله ﷺ قال: «آخر من يدخل الجنة: رجل، فهو يمشي مرة، ويكبو أخرى، وتسعفه النار مرة، فإذا ما جاوزها.. التفت إليها فقال: تبارك الذي نجاني منك، لقد أعطاني الله شيئا ما أعطاه أحدا من الأولين والآخرين.

فترفع له شجرة، فيقول: أي رب؛ أدنني من هذه الشجرة لأستظل بظلّها، وأشرب من مائها، فيقول الله: يا بن آدم، لعلي إن أعطيتكها.. تسألني غيرها، فيقول: لا يا رب.

ويعاهده ألا يسأله غيرها، وربه يعذره، لأنه يرى ما لا صبر له عليه، فيدنيه منها، فيستظل بظلها، ويشرب من مائها.

ثم ترفع له شجرة هي أحسن من الأولى، فيقول: أي رب، أدنني من هذه الشجرة لأشرب من مائها، وأستظل بظلها، ولا أسألك غيرها، فيقول: يا بن آدم، ألم تعاهدني ألا تسألني غيرها؟! فيقول: لعلي إن أدنيتك منها.. تسألني غيرها.

فيعاهده ألا يسأله غيرها، وربه يعذره؛ لأنه يرى ما لا صبر له عليه، فيدنيه منها، فيستظل بظلها، ويشرب من مائها.
ثم ترفع له شجرة عند باب الجنة هي أحسن من الأوليين، فيقول: أي رب؛ أدنني

Adam, did you not already promise Me that you would not ask me for anything else?' He will respond, 'I did, My Lord. But I will not ask You for anything else after this request.' His Lord will excuse him, as He knows that the man has seen something he cannot resist. Allah will then bring the man to the tree. When he is at the tree, he will hear the voices of the inhabitants of Paradise. He will plead, 'My Lord, let me enter it.' Allah will then say, 'What will make you stop asking Me? Will it please you if I give the whole world twice over?' He will reply, 'My Lord, do You mock me despite being the Lord of the Worlds?'

When narrating this Hadith to his students, Ibn Mas'ūd ﷺ laughed and asked, 'Why do you not ask me why I laugh?' His companions asked, 'Why are you laughing?' and he replied:

This is how the Messenger of Allah ﷺ laughed, so his Companions asked him, 'Why do you laugh, O Messenger of Allah?' He replied, 'Because when he asks, "Do You mock me despite being the Lord of the Worlds?" the Lord of the Worlds will laugh and say, "I am not mocking you. I can do whatever I want!"'

من هذه لأستظل بظلها، وأشرب من مائها، لا أسألك غيرها، فيقول: يا بن آدم؛ ألم تعاهدني ألا تسألني غيرها؟!

قال: بلى يا رب؛ هذه لا أسألك غيرها، وربه يعذره؛ لأنه يرى ما لا صبر له عليه، فيدنيه منها، فإذا أدناه منها.. سمع أصوات أهل الجنة، فيقول: أي رب، أدخلنيها، فيقول: ما يصريني منك أيرضيك إن أعطيتك الدنيا ومثلها معها؟ قال: يا رب؛ أتستهزئ بي وأنت رب العالمين؟!».

فضحك ابن مسعود فقال: ألا تسألوني مم أضحك؟! فقالوا: مم تضحك؟ قال: هكذا ضحك رسول الله ﷺ، فقالوا: مم تضحك يا رسول الله؟ قال: «من ضحك رب العالمين حين قال: أتستهزئ مني وأنت رب العالمين؟ فيقول: إني لا أستهزئ منك، ولكني على ما أشاء قادر».

Epilogue:
The Company of the Prophet ﷺ in Paradise

Know that the most noble station in Paradise is to be with our Prophet ﷺ and accompany him. It is related in a Hadith that 'Ā'ishah ؓ said:

A man came to the Messenger of Allah ﷺ and said, 'O Messenger of Allah, you are more beloved to me than my wife, myself, and my children. Sometimes when I am at home and remember you, I become so restless that I have to come and look at you. When I remember that both you and I will die, I come to the realization that you will be raised with the Prophets while I, even if I do enter Paradise, may not see you.' The Prophet ﷺ did not respond to him until Jibrīl came to him with the following verse: 'And whoever obeys Allah and the Messenger will be in the company of those blessed by Allah: the Prophets, the people of truth, the martyrs, and the righteous – what honourable company!'[69]

This Hadith conveys wonderous glad tidings and an immense reward for anyone who has complete love for the Prophet ﷺ as well as the other Prophets ﷺ and the righteous people (*ṣāliḥūn*). Love for them is a sign of one's love for Allah ﷻ. If a servant's love for Allah ﷻ is strong, his love for His friends (*awliyā'*) and righteous servants will likewise be strong.

A man once asked the Prophet ﷺ, 'What if a man loves a people but cannot reach them?' He replied, 'A man will be with those he loves.'

---

69 *al-Nisā'*, 69.

الخاتمة
في ذكر المعية النبوية في الجنة

اعلم: أن أشرف مقام في الجنة هو معية نبينا ﷺ ومرافقته، وقد جاء في الحديث عن عائشة رضي الله تعالى عنها قالت: (جاء رجل إلى رسول الله ﷺ فقال: يا رسول الله؛ إنك لأحب إلي من أهلي ومن نفسي ومن ولدي، وإني لأكون في البيت فأذكرك، وما أصبر حتى آتيك فأنظر إليك، فإذا ذكرت موتي وموتك.. عرفت أنك إذا دخلت الجنة.. رفعت مع النبيين، وإني إذا دخلت الجنة.. خشيت ألا أراك.

فلم يرد عليه شيئاً حتى نزل جبريل بهذه الآية: ﴿وَمَن يُطِعِ ٱللَّهَ وَٱلرَّسُولَ فَأُو۟لَٰٓئِكَ مَعَ ٱلَّذِينَ أَنْعَمَ ٱللَّهُ عَلَيْهِم مِّنَ ٱلنَّبِيِّـۧنَ وَٱلصِّدِّيقِينَ وَٱلشُّهَدَآءِ وَٱلصَّٰلِحِينَ وَحَسُنَ أُو۟لَٰٓئِكَ رَفِيقًا ۝٦٩﴾.

فهذا الحديث يتضمن البشارة العظيمة بالمثوبة الجسيمة لمن كملت محبته للنبي ﷺ، وكذلك من أحب غيره من سائر النبيين والصالحين؛ لأن ذلك دليل على محبة الله عز وجل. فمتى قويت محبة العبد لله تعالى.. قويت محبته لأوليائه والصالحين من عباده. وقد سأل رجل النبي ﷺ فقال له: كيف ترى في رجل أحب قوماً ولم يلحق بهم؟ قال: «المرء مع من أحب».

Another man asked him about the Hour. The Prophet ﷺ asked him, 'What have you prepared for it?' He replied, 'Nothing, besides the fact that I love Allah and His Messenger,' to which the Prophet ﷺ responded, 'You will be with those whom you love.'

Anas ؓ commented on this, saying 'In that case, I love the Prophet ﷺ, Abū Bakr, and 'Umar. It is my hope that I will be with them because of my love for them, despite my deeds not being like theirs.'

The love the Companions ؓ had for the Prophet ﷺ was of the highest order. It is narrated that there was a woman from the Anṣār whose brother and husband were killed at the Battle of Uḥud while fighting with the Messenger of Allah ﷺ. Nevertheless, she only asked 'What happened to the Messenger of Allah ﷺ?' The Companions ؓ replied, 'He is fine', whereupon she said, 'Let me see him.' When she saw him, she said, 'Any calamity is minor in comparison to losing you.'

'Amr ibn al-'Āṣ ؓ said, 'There was nobody more beloved to me than the Messenger of Allah ﷺ.'

'Alī ؓ said, 'The Messenger of Allah ﷺ was more beloved to us than our wealth, our children, our mothers, and cold water is when thirsty.'

A person should know the signs of this love so that they can strive to attain and internalise it. Some of these signs follow below:

If a person had the choice between losing one of their most prized possessions and losing the ability to see the Prophet ﷺ if it were possible, and the thought of losing his ability to see the Prophet ﷺ is more painful to him than losing that possession, that is a sign that the person has the aforementioned attribute of sincere love for the Messenger of Allah ﷺ. If he does not have this attribute, then this means that he does not have this sincere love.

وسأله آخر عن الساعة قال: «وما أعددت لها؟» قال: لا شيء، غير أني أحب الله ورسوله، قال: «أنت مع من أحببت». قال أنس: فما فرحنا بشيء فرحنا بقول رسول الله ﷺ: «أنت مع من أحببت». قال أنس: (فأنا أحب النبي ﷺ، وأبا بكر، وعمر، وأرجو أن أكون معهم بحبي إياهم، وإن لم أعمل بمثل أعمالهم).

وقد بلغ الصحابة رضوان الله عليهم في محبته ﷺ منتهى الغاية وأقصى النهاية.

ويشهد لذلك ما روي: (أن امرأة من الأنصار قتل أخوها وزوجها يوم أحد مع رسول الله ﷺ، فقالت: ما فعل رسول الله ﷺ؟ قالوا: خيراً، هو كما تحبين، فقالت: أرونيه حتى أنظر إليه. فلما رأته.. قالت: كل مصيبة بعدك جلل) يعني: صغيرة.

وقال عمرو بن العاص رضي الله عنه: (ما كان أحد أحب إلي من رسول الله ﷺ). وقال علي رضي الله عنه: (كان رسول الله ﷺ أحب إلينا من أموالنا وأولادنا وأمهاتنا، ومن الماء البارد على الظمأ).

ولابد من معرفة علامات هذه المحبة؛ ليسعى الإنسان في تحقيقها وتطبيعها.

فمنها: أن يعرض الإنسان على نفسه: أنه لو خير فقد غرض من أغراضه وفقد رؤية النبي ﷺ أن لو كانت ممكنة: فإن كان فقدها أن لو كانت ممكنة أشد عليه من فقد شيء من أغراضه.. فقد اتصف بالأحبية المذكورة لرسول الله ﷺ ومن لا.. فلا. إنتهى.

One of the greatest signs that a person truly loves the Messenger of Allah ﷺ is that they emulate him, follow his Sunnah, walk his path, model themselves on his guidance and character, and stay within the limits of his Sharī'ah. This is indicated by a Hadith narrated by al-Tirmidhī ﷺ that Anas ﷺ narrated that the Prophet ﷺ said, 'Whoever revives my Sunnah loves me, and whoever loves me will be with me in Paradise.'

Another sign that someone loves the Prophet ﷺ is that they submit to whatever he has legislated for us, and do not feel burdened by what he has ordained. They give victory to his religion through their words and actions; they defend his Sharī'ah; and adorn themselves with his qualities of generosity, preferring others over themselves, clemency, forbearance, humility, and other noble qualities.

Other signs include remembering him ﷺ abundantly, loving his Sunnah, reading his Hadith, finding pleasure in his noble remembrance, and becoming enraptured whenever one hears his sublime name.

Revering him ﷺ whenever he is mentioned and displaying submission and brokenness whenever his name is heard. Anyone who loves something is humbled by it, and many of the Companions ﷺ would become humbled whenever they mentioned his name; their skins and hearts would tremble, and they would cry. Many of the Successors ﷺ after them were also like this. Whenever Ayyūb al-Sakhtiyānī ﷺ mentioned the Prophet ﷺ, he would cry so much that those with him would pity him. Ja'far ibn Muhammad ﷺ would joke and smile frequently, but if the Prophet ﷺ was mentioned in his presence, his skin would go pale. Whenever the Prophet ﷺ was mentioned in front of 'Abd al-Raḥmān ibn al-Qāsim ﷺ his complexion would change to the extent that it was as if all the blood had drained out of him, and his tongue would become dry out of awe for

ومن أعظم العلامات لمحبة رسول الله ﷺ أيضاً: الإقتداء به، واستعمال سنته، وسلوك طريقته، والإهتداء بهديه وسيرته، والوقوف مع ما حدّ لنا من شريعته.

ويدل لذلك: ما رواه الترمذي عن أنس ﵁ مرفوعاً: «من أحيا سنتي.. فقد أحبني، ومن أحبني.. كان معي في الجنة».

ومن علامات محبته ﷺ: أن يرضى مدعيها بما شرعه حتى لا يجد في نفسه حرجاً مما قضى؛ ونصر دينه بالقول والفعل، والذب عن شريعته، والتخلق بأخلاقه في الجود، والإيثار، والحلم، والصبر، والتواضع، وغيرها من أخلاقه العظيمة.

ومنها: كثرة ذكره ﷺ، ومحبة سنته، وقراءة حديثه، وأن يلتذ بذكره الشريف، ويطرب عند سماع اسمه المنيف.

ومنها: تعظيمه ﷺ عند ذكره، وإظهار الخضوع والانكسار والخشوع مع سماع اسمه، فكل من أحب شيئاً.. خضع له كما كان كثير من الصحابة ﵃؛ إذا ذكروه.. خضعوا، واقشعرت جلودهم وبكوا.

وكذلك كان كثير من التابعين فمن بعدهم؛ فكان أيوب السختياني إذا ذكر النبي ﷺ.. بكى حتى يرحمه جلساؤه، وكان جعفر بن محمد كثير الدعابة والتبسم، فإذا ذكر النبي ﷺ عنده.. اصفر لونه، وكان عبد الرحمٰن بن القاسم إذا ذكر النبي ﷺ أمامه.. ينظر إلى لونه كأنه قد نزف منه الدم، وقد جف لسانه في فمه؛ هيبة لرسول

the Messenger of Allah ﷺ. Whenever Qatādah ؓ heard a Hadith, he would become overcome by weeping and commotion.

Another sign that someone loves him is that they love the Qur'an that he brought, guided others with and was guided by, and whose message he embodied. If you want to know how much you – or anyone else – truly loves Allah ﷻ and His Messenger ﷺ, see how much your heart loves the Qur'an and takes delight in listening to it. Is it greater than the pleasure derived by listening to musical songs? It is a well-known fact that when someone loves anything, speech concerning that thing is the most beloved topic of conversation to the one who loves it.

It is narrated that 'Uthmān ibn 'Affān ؓ said, 'If our hearts were pure, they would never have enough of the speech of Allah.' How can a lover ever have enough of his beloved's speech when it is the pinnacle of what they desire? Whenever Abū Mūsā ؓ was with a group of the Companions ؓ they would ask him, 'O Abū Mūsā ؓ, remind us of our Lord.' He would then recite the Qur'an while they listened.

Another sign is that one yearns to meet him ﷺ, since every lover yearns to meet their beloved. Some even say that the very definition of love is yearning for one's beloved. For this reason, whenever the Companions ؓ experienced an intense longing, they would seek out the Messenger of Allah ﷺ. They would find respite by simply looking at him, deriving pleasure by being in his company, looking at him, and seeking his ﷺ blessings (barakah).

'Abdah bint Khālid ibn Ma'dān ؓ narrated:

Whenever Khālid laid down to sleep, he would remember his longing for the Messenger of Allah ﷺ and his Companions from the Muhājirūn and Anṣār. He would mention them by name and say, 'They are my ancestry (aṣl) as well as my progeny (faṣl); for them does my heart long. Long has been my yearning for them. My Lord, hasten Your seizing of my soul unto You!' until he would fall asleep.

الله ﷺ، وكان قتادة إذا سمع الحديث.. أخذه العويل والزويل.

ومنها: حب القرآن الذي أتى به، وهدى به، واهتدى به، وتخلق به، وإذا أردت أن تعرف ما عندك وعند غيرك من محبة الله ورسوله.. فانظر محبة القرآن من قلبك، والتذاذك بسماعه أهو أعظم من التذاذ أصحاب الملاهي والغناء المطرب بسماعهم؟

فإنه من المعلوم: من أحب محبوباً.. كان كلامه وحديثه أحب شيء إليه.

ويروى: أن عثمان بن عفان ﵁ قال: (لو طهرت قلوبنا.. ما شبعنا من كلام الله؟!)، وكيف يشبع المحب من كلام محبوبه وهو غاية مطلوبه؟ وكان الصحابة رضي الله عنهم إذا اجتمعوا وفيهم أبو موسى.. يقولون: يا أبا موسى؛ ذكرنا ربنا، فيقرأ وهم يسمعون.

ومنها: كثرة الشوق إلى لقائه ﷺ؛ إذ كل حبيب يحب لقاء حبيبه.
قال بعضهم: (المحبة): الشوق إلى المحبوب. ولهذا كان الصحابة ﵏ إذا اشتد بهم الشوق.. قصدوا رسول الله ﷺ، واستشفوا بمشاهدته، وتلذذوا بالجلوس والنظر إليه، والتبرك به ﷺ.

وعن عبدة بنت خالد بن معدان قالت: ما كان خالد يأوي إلى فراشه إلا وهو يذكر من شوقه إلى رسول الله ﷺ، وإلى أصحابه من المهاجرين والأنصار؛ يسميهم ويقول: (بهم أصلي وفصلي، وإليهم يحن قلبي، طال شوقي إليهم، فعجّل رب قبضي إليك)

When Bilāl ﷺ was dying, his wife cried out, 'O woe!' He responded, 'O joy! Tomorrow I shall meet the beloved ones – Muhammad and his Fellowship!'

O Allah ﷻ, enable us with an enabling grace that will prevent us from disobeying You, and prompt us to do that which brings about Your contentment for us. Allow us to prepare for what You have promised us. Continue to bless us with Your beneficence that You have made us so accustomed to. Complete the honour You have bestowed upon us and forgive us, our parents and all the Muslims, by Your Mercy, O Most Merciful of those that are merciful!

Sayyid Muhammad ibn ʿAlawī al-Mālikī ﷺ

حتى يغلبه النوم. ولما احتضر بلال.. نادت امرأته: وا ويلاه ! فقال: (وا طرباه ! غدا ألقى الأحبه، محمداً وحزبه).

اللهم؛ وفقنا توفيقاً يوقفنا عن معاصيك، ويحثنا للإقبال لما يرضيك، وارزقنا الاستعداد لما وعدتنا، وأدم لنا احسانك كما عودتنا، وأتمم علينا ما به أكرمتنا، واغفر لنا ولوالدينا ولجميع المسلمين، برحمتك يا أرحم الراحمين.

السيد محمد بن علوي المالكي